Business-driven Research and Development

Managing Knowledge to Create Wealth

Dr Ashok Ganguly

MACMILLAN
Business

First published 1999 by
MACMILLAN PRESS LTD
Houndmills, Basingstoke, Hampshire RG21 6XS
and London
Companies and representatives
throughout the world

ISBN 0–333–77650–X hardcover

A catalogue record for this book is available
from the British Library.

This book is printed on paper suitable for recycling and
made from fully managed and sustained forest sources.

10 9   8   7   6 5   4   3   2   1
08 07 06 05 04 03 02 01 00 99

Editing and origination by
Aardvark Editorial, Mendham, Suffolk

Printed and bound in Great Britain by
Creative Print & Design (Wales), Ebbw Vale

For Connie, Nivedita and Amrita

Contents

Prologue

Why I decided to write a book on R&D in industry and why people should be interested in it needs some explanation. In many businesses, and even in the so-called high technology ones, the eyes of CEOs and senior executives have been known to start to glaze over whenever the topic of discussions turns to R&D. This reaction may be traced back to widespread dissatisfaction with R&D in industry, especially in the 1970s and 80s. The only exceptions are among R&D-based start-ups, sponsored by venture capital companies, in areas ranging from IT and genetics to pharmaceuticals and telephonics. Published statistics suggest that while most firms steadily invest in R&D as a measure to enhance shareholder value, entrepreneurial start-ups, originating from scientific ideas and breakthroughs, tend to earmark a larger percentage of their funds to R&D. In developing economies R&D in industry is generally non-existent leading to some serious consequences, which are now widely known.

I began my professional career as a scientist in an industrial R&D laboratory of a multinational subsidiary in India. In due course, I moved to manufacturing and, eventually, became the chairman of the MNC's (multinational corporation's) subsidiary in India. The survival of this Indian subsidiary in the 1960s and 70s was heavily dependent upon import substitution of its key raw material. My understanding of business-driven R&D originated in the successful import substitution efforts of this MNC subsidiary. This company, as a result of its early R&D success, became the largest and most successful foreign company in India. In the course of my working career, through various interactions with the parent MNC as well as actual work experience in Europe and America, I began to notice a growing disenchantment of the business with its R&D, especially during the 1970s and 80s. In due course, I became aware that effectiveness of R&D in industry was an issue of wider concern among many companies in the USA as well as across Europe during these two decades. Thus in 1990, when I was appointed as an Executive Director on the Main Board of the MNC and made responsible for research and technology, the tensions between business and R&D in the company were fairly palpable. This was about the same time as the IT explosion was beginning to spread, although its impact on business was becoming noticeable mainly in the banking and financial services sector. Simultaneously, the emergence of knowledge management as a formal process had started to be more widely perceived, especially for its impact on business competitiveness and in the creation of wealth.

The imperative to change some of the traditional business beliefs and practices was thus becoming obvious and the lack of connection between R&D and the marketplace was identified as a key weakness by many business enterprises. The only way a connection between these could be established required the joint efforts of business heads and R&D managers. The prerequisite for establishing a wealth-creating connection between the marketplace and R&D demanded a much more profound understanding of consumers/customers in different markets than ever before in the history of modern commerce, while at the same time radically changing the management of R&D and making it an unambiguous business-relevant process. Because these developments were a consequence of an emerging business environment, and therefore had a direct effect on business performance, the readiness to change traditional views, attitudes and work practices was already widely prevalent in our organisation. During the 1990s I also came across examples of similar changes in business-driven relationships taking place in many other companies across Europe and in the USA. On the other hand, in Japanese industries, SBU heads and their R&D colleagues have traditionally tended to work together comparatively more intimately and were therefore somewhat better placed. As in the case of most management advances, the concept of business–R&D intimacy was rapidly adapted across companies in the USA. However, in Europe there still remain a few pockets of resistance. The R&D director of a very large and venerable European MNC in the electrical and electronic business was convinced that he had a 'responsibility' to protect R&D from undue business 'interference'. He had developed arguments to prove that the value of the patents generated in the company's R&D laboratories, in his charge, represented several-fold potential returns when measured against the company's investment in R&D. It was another matter that his claims could not be related to business performance of the MNC which happened to be on a downward spiral. In my subsequent encounters with other R&D directors, for example in industry R&D associations in Europe, I found that such attitudes and views as

I have described above were more widely held than one had expected. Fortunately, however, among the vast majority of American and European industries, including the one I was employed in, business managers as well as R&D managers were committed to abandon traditional practices and seek new ways to drive R&D, and thus to achieve specific business objectives.

I was particularly fortunate to have among my most senior research colleagues individuals who turned out to be the principal advocates for the introduction of the new business-driven R&D management process. Incidentally, in our case, the business-driven R&D initiative also called for dismantling geographical and cultural barriers and from that, as a consequence, was born the concept of *borderless laboratories*.

Most of the issues described above are not likely to appear as being novel to most managers in industry. In spite of this, two reasons persuaded me to write this book. The first is that while there is a general acceptance of the view that business heads and their R&D colleagues need to work closely together in order to derive competitive advantages, most of the published literature describing the ways of achieving this objective happen to be too amorphous to be effective in practice. The second, and probably even more compelling, reason was the amazing transformation which started to take place among scientists in our laboratories following the adaptation of a formal business-driven R&D process. Once the business-driven R&D processes started falling in place, the vast majority of my scientist colleagues turned out to be the most ardent advocates of the new ways of working. Our research laboratories became infused with a new sense of purpose, while individual scientists began to exude high levels of enthusiasm and energy. The root cause for all this excitement and enthusiasm in the laboratories was that the business-driven R&D process enabled the employees to relate their R&D work to clear business objectives. Shifting from hierarchical organisation structures to working in project teams further clarified the role and accountability of individual research scientists, at all levels, as never before. Ultimately the changes brought about by business-driven R&D were seen as being highly motivating by all the individuals involved, whether in the research laboratories or in the operating companies.

Research scientists no longer waited, apprehensively, for the annual funding round, preparing defences to ward off threats to their pet projects and programmes. Business heads took their role as custodians of their research programmes very seriously, since the future of their business depended upon the success of the R&D projects. In this process, investment in fundamental research also could now be clearly linked to the long-term strategy of business, as indeed were the related scientific partnerships with academia and other external institutions.

The rapid spread of IT had an extremely timely and a most profound influence on business-driven R&D. It helped establish and infuse a highly dynamic and productive innovation culture across the company's geographical spread, linking subsidiaries and operating companies with the help of world-wide IT networks.

The methodologies needed to usher in a business-driven R&D culture in a company are now reasonably well established. From the descriptions in the following chapters in this book, it should be reasonably easy for a firm to adopt processes best suited to its markets and technologies, provided a firm is mentally and culturally prepared to usher in such change. All world-class businesses are already being driven by advances in technology and new knowledge. The half-life of new innovations is rapidly dwindling. In order to sustain market leadership, combining superior consumer understanding, innovation and R&D have become indispensable for business continuity and success. It is therefore no surprise that innovation and technology now figure prominently in the agenda of corporate board deliberations and most CEOs have taken charge and become key sponsors of these changes in their companies.

Improvements in methods and processes for managing R&D in industry will, of course, continue as indeed they should. This book, which began in the early 1990s, is an attempt to describe a small step in that process.

Acknowledgements

I am grateful to all my colleagues on the Board of Unilever, who were instrumental in helping me develop the concept of business-driven R&D. However, Mr Jan Peelen and Mr Anthony Burgmans were particularly influential in encouraging me, from the very start, to explore ways and means to weave together business priorities and research programmes in the businesses they headed. The three of us worked together, from the beginning, to develop the concept of business-driven R&D. The concept was so simple, while at the same time so compelling, that in due course other parts of the business readily adopted the new methodologies. In establishing a formal innovation management process described in Chapter 5, we were greatly helped and guided by Professor Kim Clark and his colleague Eric Mankin of Integral Corpn. Among my most senior research colleagues Drs Tom Little, Hans Nieuwenhuis, Roger Platt, Lincoln Krochmal, Ray Moran, Alan Mckinnon, Anthony Lee, Alan Evanson, Jan de Rooj, Alistaire Pennman and Jeroon Bordwijk became the most enthusiastic drivers and agents of change. Ms Erika Jones, of Erika Jones and Associates, helped lay the foundation stone for the project team building and project team training programmes described in Chapter 7 which turned out to be a decisive factor for success. Rob Daniel, a senior HR Manager in R&D, was put in charge, and helped launch the new training programmes and prepare the training manuals.

The availability of a user-friendly IT support system turned out to be the second most important success factor. Dr David Frost was responsible for creation of the IT framework described in Chapter 6 which facilitated the project team management process and also laid the foundation for the creation of the world-wide innovation network. It is inevitable that in this brief account it is not possible to acknowledge many others, without whose vital inputs and commitment the concept of business-driven R&D would have remained attractive as an idea rather than becoming a reality. Literally hundreds of employees across our research laboratories, innovation centres and operating companies made these processes alive by application in their day-to-day work. Last but not least, I acknowledge with gratitude the patience and diligence with which my secretary, Mrs Amy Bharda, typed what at times seemed to be endless drafts of the manuscript.

Preface

The *aim* of this book is to share with readers in industry and academia, as well as with policy makers, my experience and learning as to how science and technology may be managed more purposefully in industry in order to meet well-defined business objectives. Two books were written, by business consultants, on the subject in the 1990s – P A Roussel, K N Saad, and T J Erickson, *Third Generation R&D* (1991), Harvard Business School Press; J V Buckley, *Going for Growth* (1998) New York, McGraw-Hill. Both books contain good descriptions of some of the contemporary industrial R&D and business management issues. As a matter of fact, of the two books, *Third Generation R&D* comes somewhat closer in describing certain real issues in industry. But both texts miss the practical perspective of day-to-day problems of managing R&D in an industrial environment. Furthermore, these books do not deal sufficiently with certain important topics such as the role of human resources, IT, academic linkages and several others which have profound influence on the effectiveness of industrial R&D. These are omissions which are also fairly common in research and review papers published in journals on the subject during the past 10–15 years. This led me to conclude that what had been described in the above two books, as well as some other publications, compared to the reality of an industrial work environment, was significantly diverse. Such gaps in the comprehension of industrial R&D could only be filled by relating certain firm-level experiences.

The *scope* of the book is built around the fundamental premise that in industry the primary role of R&D is to fulfil business objectives within a framework of time and cost targets. R&D in industry is, however, unlike any other business service function. While the formulation of business objectives is the prime responsibility of business managers, the chances of achieving such objectives can be significantly improved if done jointly with R&D managers. This way of joint working assumes certain competencies among business and R&D managers, in order to understand the changing nature of markets and the power of R&D to deal with them. It, of course, does not work this way in all firms. IBM in the 1980s and Philips in the 1990s, two prominent companies, owned two of the most prestigious industrial R&D set-ups in the world. Such was the quality of their research that some of their scientists even shared the Nobel prize for their discoveries. Yet both businesses suffered badly – IBM in the 1980s, Philips in the 1990s – primarily because of the vast gap between what customers and consumers were asking for from these firms, as compared to the type of projects their marketing and R&D departments were engaged in. My book's *aim* is to describe some of the reasons as to how and why such gaps develop and what steps may be taken to avoid them.

In the course of exploring the key reasons for the disjunction between R&D and the marketplace, as well as explaining how firms may ensure that such discontinuities may be avoided, the *scope* of the book in *certain related* areas has logically been extended. Description of these areas provides a holistic model of how *business-driven R&D* may be managed to derive sustainable competitive advantage.

One such area is related to the phenomenal spread of education in the developed countries. A consequence of this diffusion is that generating and managing knowledge have emerged as prominent competitive forces for industry and academia as well as for countries. Knowledge links industry, universities and national governments in different ways in order to create wealth; some of these ways are very new, and many of them are not yet well understood. Understanding the power of knowledge management is critical in modernising and driving industrial R&D. Consequently, it is attracting increasing interest from researchers as well as from national governments. Chapter 3 is devoted to the subject of knowledge and some of its impact on *business-driven R&D*.

A second area concerns human resource (HR) development, primarily as it relates to scientists in industry. Historically, this has been a neglected area of management attention. Many of the traditional attitudes, disappointments and disjunctions between industrial R&D and business can be directly attributed to incomplete appreciation of the human resource issues. In course of exploring this subject it was discovered that specially designed HR strategies can dramatically transform the work environment and attitude of scientists in industrial R&D laboratories. Furthermore, these strategies also trigger attitudinal changes in the rest of a corporation with some remarkable consequences. Progressively, R&D and business managers begin working in new ways and enrich the impact of science on business performance. Interestingly, this new HR initiative also spreads beyond the firm level and facilitates new types of partnerships with universities and other research institutions As a consequence, such partnerships become sustainable and more productive for the participants in ways which were not achievable previously. Another consequence is that organisation structures in firms begin to change, as well, in order to reflect the new ways of working. Such new HR-driven changes are taking place faster in some corporations than others. But the general trend in most major corporations, in the developed world, is more or less similar to what is described in Chapter 7.

The third area concerns the management of innovation with the help of firm-level innovation networks. Such networks have to be formally set up in a company in order to facilitate communication between operating companies (the interface with consumers/customers), the corporate headquarters (agreeing priorities) and central R&D (using science and technology to drive innovation). This way of networking has only become possible because of advances in IT and telephony. The development and adaptation of user-friendly and task-dedicated software now enables round-the-clock traffic across a firm's knowledge highway. Such a knowledge highway, in turn, permanently and positively influences a company's work culture, managerial attitudes and the speed of response to unmet market needs and new opportunities. The dynamics as well as the sustainability of a firm's knowledge network eventually determine its business performance. In this respect, some of the most profound changes are taking place in the pharmaceutical and electronic industries. The roles of internal as well as external knowledge sources have already begun to change the nature of these two industries dramatically (Chapter 9). Chapters 3, 4, 5 and 9 include a brief survey of literature, the impact of globalisation of business and some other related topics such as risk management, and so on.

I have been planning to write this book since 1997. As far as I am aware the subject has not been addressed by any other industrial R&D practitioner in the recent past. I have learnt some very valuable lessons as a head of a major industrial R&D set-up and wish to share these with a wider audience, without infringing on any confidential corporate issues to which I may be privy.

1 Introduction – What is Business-driven R&D?

The changes in the marketplace in the 1990s, brought about by the twin forces of globalisation and the end of the era of cold war, are even more profound compared to the re-emergence of new market forces after World War II. This book is concerned with issues which are influencing the conduct of scientific research both in universities and in industry, as they have a major influence on the current developments in the marketplaces around the world. The rapidly growing importance of knowledge as the new currency for economic and social development has pushed science much more into the public domain and, as a consequence, has generated unprecedented demands for accountability and overall social relevance. The practice of curiosity-driven, blue-sky scientific enquiry, emanating from fundamental human curiosity, is now being required to be better balanced by the needs of wealth creation, employment generation, social justice and the care of the environment in which we live.

In view of the rapid advances in every sphere of science and technology and their increasingly visible impact on human society, and particularly in the conduct of business and commerce, some developments both in academia and in industry have turned out to be a rich source of learning and hence worthwhile recording. It is from this basic premise that the concept of a text describing business-driven R&D emerged. Business has traditionally been one of the principal means of generating wealth and employment. What has become explicit is that a more systematic and purposeful approach to the generation and management of knowledge significantly raises the competitive advantages in a business. The strategy, planning, funding and management of R&D in a business happen to be one of the principal sources for generating new knowledge. In a business-driven R&D culture, it has been found that the coupling of R&D with

1

markets is what differentiates many of today's corporations from their predecessors. IBM is probably the best contemporary example of a business which was able to revive its fortunes by coupling its technological wealth with the opportunities in the marketplace. As a result, this successfully brought about a critical cultural transformation in the corporation. In contrast, Philips is still struggling to seek a somewhat similar transformation, but has been much slower to achieve satisfactory end results.

The concept of business-driven exploitation of science and technology is critically important for all modern businesses. However, other than occasional case studies of individual corporations, a unified picture of this new paradigm has not yet been described in a manner so as to make the process widely understood and applicable. In the next chapter a brief review of some recent literature on the subject reveals that important gaps between the theory and practice of managing R&D in industry still persist. Unfortunately, in industry the traditional conflict between the compulsions of secrecy, especially when issues of proprietary technology and intellectual property are concerned, and the need to record good practices has never been satisfactorily resolved. It is, however, both proper and possible to describe successful business experiences of good R&D management practice, without transcending corporate confidentiality, and this has been strictly adhered to in the preparation of this book.

On the other hand, it is quite a common practice among academics and industrial researchers to exchange experiences openly when they deliberate in government committees appointed to discuss effectiveness of R&D funding. Best practices are readily and openly shared among committee members regarding the choice of funding priorities and assessing economic multipliers resulting from government investments in R&D. The proceedings of such deliberations become the subject of government records but, barring a few exceptions, generally remain outside the public domain and rarely become accessible for wider dissemination and use, either by industry or in universities. In effect, every time such new committees are constituted by government, they tend to begin their deliberations from square one. This is another reason why the results of successful interaction between universities and industry on science policy need to be recorded and analysed for wider dissemination and use.

The present text, while not attempting solely to collate examples from current literature on R&D management and policy, draws heavily from a wide array of the best practices in different countries, as reported in published literature, and blends them with the hands-on management experiences of the author. Key conclusions are based upon some benchmarking comparisons with other industries.

As a result of such an approach, certain issues emerged which are described in some detail in the different chapters of this book. These issues may be briefly summarised as follows:

- Due to growth of modern interactive communication and technology, the comprehension of the results of even very complex scientific discoveries is now fairly widespread, not only among the public in general, but even more so among CEOs and business managers. As a consequence, business managers and CEOs are today more easily able to relate their investments in R&D to specific market opportunities, as compared to their predecessors.

- It is becoming progressively clear that coupling the discipline of business management with R&D management need not necessarily curb creativity. As a matter of fact, it is now being widely recognised in industry that scientific creativity in isolation, no matter how outstanding and original, unless managed in a framework of business discipline, can lead to waste and chaos.

- Big scientific breakthroughs can no longer be achieved by individuals working in isolation. Most modern scientific and technological breakthroughs are being achieved by the efforts of multidisciplinary teams. It has been found that exceptional leadership as well as individual excellence and accountability, even when working in teams, are prerequisites of successful and productive team dynamics.

- The language of the marketplace and the language of scientific enquiry are now merging as a result of growing interactions between businessmen and managers of R&D. Their common goal is jointly to generate competitive advantages for firms. This is valid not only for near-market R&D projects but even in the choice of areas of fundamental scientific research, which are long term by their very nature.

- Interweaving of business and R&D is taking place simultaneously, while new methodologies and techniques are being devised by marketing specialists to interpret the messages derived from exploring consumer needs and demands. Interpreting consumer needs, and then initiating anticipatory scientific exploration to exploit such new opportunities, is enabling firms to develop proprietary technology, and build consumer-relevant attributes into goods and services, ahead of competitors.

■ The ability continuously to capture precise marketplace knowledge helps to define business priorities with greater clarity. Business priorities are problems whose successful solution generates competitive advantages. In order to solve such business problems they are usually broken down into discrete components. These components are then converted into scientific theory-based, and hypothesis-driven, projects. The end results, in turn, drive a firm's innovation engine. In the absence of such a disciplined approach, problem definition, in terms of business opportunity, tends to be vague and scientific approaches to find solutions turn out to be highly empirical and unnecessarily risky. Such dissonance is the root cause for the traditional disjunction between business and R&D managers in the vast majority of firms.

■ Training and development of scientific manpower to understand and manage R&D in industry is probably the single most important success factor. Unfortunately, the subject has remained grossly neglected and unexplored. Scientists recruited into industry R&D laboratories tend to have very superficial understanding of business processes, of market dynamics, or for that matter how any business is managed. Traditionally, training to work as scientists or managers of science in industry is not imparted in universities and has a peripheral place in most management schools. Formal learning of how a business works, and how wealth is created by it, is critical to the effectiveness of newly recruited scientists who join R&D departments in industry. Such learning has to be supplemented by formal training in industry to work in teams, in order to plan and execute real-life business projects. Well-planned and well-crafted formal induction and training of scientists joining industry has been found to produce spectacular results in a business while, at the same time, releasing enormous intellectual and creative energy among scientists who choose a career in industrial R&D.

■ Human resource management is now considered a core activity in industrial R&D. Special emphasis has to be placed on precisely defining the skill and competency profiles of scientists and R&D managers, and then using these as measures in the selection and recruitment of world-class scientists. Following recruitment, in addition to formally exposing the scientists to the world of management, business and commerce, as well as to the details of a firm's business management process, they have to be formally exposed to a number of related subjects, such as leadership and team working. Subsequent steps involve formal interaction with individual scientists in order to develop their career profiles and growth paths. Such career plans, for individuals, must also include formal programmes for continuous learning, which is particularly important for scientists. Focusing at the individual scientist level incidentally also facilitates the outplacement and rehabilitation at the earliest signs of any mismatch between an individual and the organisation in the first year or two following recruitment.

■ Because of the explosive advances in every sphere of science, the traditional and individualised ways of keeping abreast of scientific interests and relevant adjacent areas can no longer ensure sufficient renewal of skills and competencies of individual scientists, no matter how talented they are. Nowadays, formal learning, at predetermined frequencies, is the only way that a scientist is able to sustain levels of skill and competency, essential for the duration of a scientifically productive working life.

■ Important changes are also taking place in the relationship between universities, research institutions and industry R&D departments. The emergence of new university–industry partnerships, by academics working on industry R&D projects in formal and joint teams, is replacing the traditional donor–recipient contracts and relations between academia and industry. Well-planned access to appropriate academic centres, which are generators of knowledge, through a network of project partnerships, is turning out to be the only cost-effective method for a firm to sustain a critical mass of leading-edge R&D capability.

■ Partnerships between universities and industry thus facilitate the establishment of a value chain, linking academic partners to a set of business-relevant scientific themes. This is done by defining outputs emanating from scientific discoveries and their ability to fuel enabling and appropriate market-relevant technologies. Such enabling technologies, in turn, are a prime resource to drive a company's business-innovation projects. Innovation projects, managed by formal innovation processes, enable corporations to connect research laboratories directly to operating companies, and thus to exploit market opportunities ahead of competitors. In this way the value-chain circle is closed within a firm, since the operating companies happen to be the initiators of business-relevant innovation projects, in the first instance.

■ To work successfully in multidisciplinary (inter and intra) teams, as well as to practise management by process, necessitates profound cultural change in most organisations. At the fundamental level, this demands a shift from the traditional hierarchical organisational structures towards flatter matrices. Such new structures are defined by tasks and accountability of individuals, as opposed to the command and control exercised by seniority and titles of earlier times. Among all such changes a shift to a business-driven R&D culture is one of the most complex and takes longer than other business processes to take root in companies. An objective system of reward and recognition, which consistently acknowledges achievements while encouraging behaviour patterns which are in tune with a business-driven R&D process, ensures consistent, leading-edge scientific breakthroughs, in a time and result-orientated business environment. Furthermore, working in dedicated project teams, without diluting individual accountability, and purposeful management of risks, generates absolute transparency and widespread acceptance of business-driven R&D among all employees in a company.

■ Probably the greatest gain is the demystification of the process of scientific enquiry for business managers, without in any way diluting the profundity of scientific exploration. Such demystification is the only way to help clarify the links between R&D and the marketplace, for both the scientist and the business managers. It also sharpens the accountability of business managers for the successful exploitation of innovations to generate competitive advantages for the firm.

This brief account, hopefully, underscores the fact that, while there may be nothing profound or unique in the concept of business-driven

R&D, the discipline necessary to shift away from traditional ways of working is considerable. However, because the concepts are simple, the tasks become relatively easy to comprehend, define and implement. From CEOs to marketing managers to research scientists, everyone becomes an important player in a business transformation process engendered in adopting a business-driven R&D culture. Consequently, the emergence of a knowledge-driven, high energy, innovation culture eventually transforms a corporation and enables it to meet the growing challenges of the marketplace and thus enhance shareholder value.

Some Gleanings from Recent Publications

Among the number of publications on industrial R&D in recent years there are certain underlying features which are worth noting. Some of these publications[1,3] include research papers which are based on extensive data from diverse industries spread across the USA, Europe and Japan – countries in which most of the industrial R&D is carried out. Incidentally, the majority of the authors of these publications have a background in social sciences, finance or management studies. Many of the investigators have attempted to fit their findings and data into different forms of unified hypothesis and mathematical formulae, in attempts to impart a quantitative rigour to their interpretations and conclusions; in contrast, some of the data represented in graphical form lack quantitative rigour which, as a consequence, detracts from their interpretative value. Some of the research is without doubt excellent. But if anyone in industry, whether an R&D manager or a finance manager, or a business head for that matter, were to try and seek useful directions to help decide R&D funding or to choose R&D priorities, most of these publications offer limited help, even if the reader persists in trying to use some of their complex equations. Finally, it is also curious that so few of the authors are either practising scientists or scientists who have moved on to become R&D managers in industry.

Though it is not entirely clear why this should be so, it is worth speculating on some of the reasons for this state of affairs. Most academic scientists of repute spend so much of their time preparing tomes for funding applications and drafting and redrafting the manuscripts of their own research results that it leaves them very little time to explore and record the process of selecting, promoting, funding and conducting scientific research itself. On the other hand, in industry there is a general preoccupation with secrecy, as well as other competitive compulsions, which discourages investigation and recording of the management process involved in industrial R&D. Normally, industry is comfortable with information to be in the public domain only if the intellectual property rights are fully protected. This attitude is to a certain extent justified when one occasionally encounters unpleasant instances of industrial espionage. While such incidents of intellectual theft may not be widespread they do reinforce the tendency to be secretive. Some industry research associations do periodically review generic trends and methodologies related to R&D management while publication of R&D spending by industries is now a regular feature in the financial press as a key source of information to shareholders and financial analysts.[4] Most such published information is useful as reference material but of limited utility in policy formulation or in management decision making. Unfortunately, in the majority of the institutions of management education, the topic of R&D management usually tends to occupy a very narrow and rarefied niche which occasionally gets sharper and more insightful in case studies published by consulting firms.

In 1972 the National Science Foundation (USA) organised a conference which was a pioneering effort to explore the links between technology and the economy. In 1994 another conference was sponsored by the NSF, to explore areas of public policy and new thrust areas in R&D for their impact on the economy in the post cold war era. Brookings and AEI, who have spearheaded R&D policy research in the USA for several decades, were the principal collaborators in organising the 1994 conference.[2] Some of the research papers presented in the 1994 conference have contemporary relevance to the subject of business-driven R&D and are worth quoting from.

Between 1972 and 1994, while the knowledge of the linkage between R&D and economic growth had advanced significantly, the complexity of the issues involved as well as the remaining gaps also increased. Thus, although certain factors are common to technical advances in virtually every sector of the economy, important differences among sectors affect the nature and the source of technical change in individual areas. For example, in aircraft and telecommunications, the end products are complex systems composed of many sub-systems and components. Technological advances may stem either from improvements in individual components or from dramatic system level redesign; in either case improvements result from the work of upstream components or material producers and system engineers. The chemical and pharmaceutical industries, on the other hand, manifest a strikingly different model. Innovations in these industries are characterised by introduction of new products, and much less of the incremental upgrading characteristic of systems technologies is evident.

Because of the complexity of the innovation process, determining precisely the qualitative or quantitative benefits to society from individual research projects has been extremely difficult, if not impossible. While at the individual firm level the benefits of R&D can now be more precisely measured, the problem arises in aggregation, both at the sector level as well as nationally. Difficulty in macro-level measurements is mainly due to the absence, until now, of measurement of academic output as well as those from defence R&D. Thus, although most researchers in the field of knowledge and wealth creation strongly suspect a positive correlation between investment in R&D and economic growth, the ability more precisely and reliably to measure the relationship has remained elusive.

Robert Solow[5] pioneered the work on growth accounting, measuring impact of research on the rate of technological change in the United States during the first half of the twentieth century. Solow concluded that 'a residual or unexplained portion of US economic growth stemmed from technological advances and this residual far outweighed changes in capital and labour'. This was confirmed by Denison[6] who estimated that 20 per cent of US economic growth between 1939 and 1957 is accounted for by R&D. Mansfield's[7] research at the University of Pennsylvania suggests that, for the period 1975–85, about 10 per cent of new products in six industries – information processing, electrical equipment, scientific instruments, drugs, metals, and oil – could not have been developed (or would have faced substantial delays) without access to contemporary academic research. Notwithstanding some of these pioneering explorations, the current state of knowledge on R&D benefits is marked by both progress and even more intellectual puzzles. In addition, there is now much public interest in the relationship between investment in R&D and economic gains. The 1994 conference[2] tried to address some of these vexing issues.

Since many of the presentations at the conference referred to different aspects of science and wealth creation in society, it is worth mentioning some of the key observations. One major underlying theme was the implicit or explicit assumption that, as we approach the closing days of this millennium, R&D, in general, is progressively and heavily needs driven and not only curiosity driven. The tension between research autonomy and social direction can be traced back to the 1930s debate in Great Britain between Michael Polanyi and J D Bernal. Polanyi stressed the need for scientific autonomy and self-governance if research were to contribute most creatively to society, while Bernal foresaw greater need for large-scale mobilisation of research to achieve explicitly formulated social goals. Brooks considers the tensions between the two approaches as healthy and unavoidable.[8]

Nelson and Romer[9] do not find cause for alarm in a more explicit orientation of universities towards the fulfilment of social needs. They are uncomfortable with the tendency of some scientists to insist almost as a matter of principle on the non-utility of their research. They further point out that some of the most interesting scientific discoveries and the most significant applications have come from work of a problem-solving character that was neither wholly curiosity driven nor wholly needs driven. In support of this, they refer to the scientific work of Pasteur. Louis Pasteur was a scientist, intensely interested in fundamental scientific concepts but whose work was heavily influenced by practical problems arising in medicine and in the industries of the day. Nelson and Romer, however, also caution the need to strive continuously for a balance between the two in order to provide a degree of flexibility and accommodation.

Boskin and Lau[10] have studied the complementarity between R&D and human capital, human capital and tangible capital, and technology and tangible capital, that produces significant interactive effects. For example, the benefits to the economy of R&D in improved micro-processors will depend on the amount of tangible capital that can make use of the faster microprocessors and on the human capital able and available to use the computers and the other forms of new technology, such as advanced software, which enhances the capabilities of the improved systems. In spite of their state-of-the-art mathematical corre-lation, Boskin and Lau conclude that 'R&D is important to economic growth, but just how important is a question economists are not yet fully able to answer'. Hall,[11] on the other hand, is sceptical of the current state of economic validation and insists on the need for more satisfying rationale for appropriate levels of R&D investment. She believes that only in this way will it be possible to decide the type of government R&D investments which are most productive and neces-sary. There is therefore an urgent need for a process that would incorporate a more explicit awareness and discussion of the broad goals to be accomplished by research in advance of performing the research, and this can only be achieved by undertaking detailed dialogue between the researchers and the end-users or customers of the research, before new research programmes are undertaken.[12] Mansfield, who has been a pioneer in the field of measuring R&D utility, has traditionally been more positive about his findings because he has focused on the industry sector where aggregation provides more clarity. He claims that high rates of return from research are more clearly evident in certain industries than in others, but across the board the social rates of return from research are substantial. While exploring links between basic research done in universities and technical advances in industry, he has found substantial evidence to support the claim that basic research has contributed to industrial innovation. Although he does not believe that any single pattern of university–industry relationship should apply in all instances, Mansfield strongly advocates closer university–industry linkages in general, and sees good reasons for those universities with traditionally close ties to certain industries and firms to go even further in this direction.[13]

Some of the key but unresolved issues which emerged during the 1994 conference[2] are relevant not only for their future impact on R&D in the USA but also in other developed and emerging economies as well. For instance, it is now amply clear that society is bound to impose stricter standards of relevance on the scientific community, independent of domestic politics and defence spending. Second, the traditional boundaries between government laboratories, industry and the universities are blurring and new opportunities as well as new vulnerabilities are emerging in the post cold war research environment. Under these conditions, even if the social returns from research are demonstrated convincingly, in analytical terms, the influence of the political process will continue to have its own logic and impact on science. The cuts by the state, that have afflicted research funding of other Western nations and countries of the former Soviet Union in recent years, have been dramatic compared with what has happened thus far in the United States. But one view is that this gives the scientific community in America a breathing space to plan for a more orderly contraction of its overall size that can be sustained in the foreseeable future. What none of the researchers argues is that this could be a reason for the continuous good performance of the US economy and the role of high technology stocks in keeping the stock markets buoyant! However, the problem of R&D funding is leading to new forms of collaborations and partnerships between various research sectors and is bound to promote greater output and creativity.

One of the important players in this changing scenario is industrial R&D. The reorganisation and reorientation of R&D in various sectors of industry as well as at the firm level remains relatively under-explored as a subject. It is essential to fill in the gaps in our understanding of the changes in industrial R&D in order for the three elements – academia, government and industrial R&D – to be inter-linked most effectively. In broad qualitative terms, the industrial element is being driven by the rise in the rate of obsolescence of new innovations, globalisation of business activities and intensification of competition.

Two books authored by business consultants in the 1990s – one in 1991[14] and the second in 1998[15] – deal with more contemporary issues related to R&D management in industry. The first and probably the most definitive account on industrial R&D in the 1990s is the trea-tise on *Third Generation R&D* by Roussel *et al.*[14] All three authors draw their experience from their consulting experience at Arthur D Little Inc. Their core conclusion is that

> the firms that succeed in global competition will be those that employ technology to maintain an edge in product quality and innovation, an advantage in production and marketing, productivity and responsive-ness to market interests.

Industrial research, as we know it at present, was started in the early twentieth century by pioneers in Europe and the USA, notwith-standing a general scepticism among businessmen who saw little connection between 'academic' science and product innovation and who valued hard assets over intellectual property. After World War II, R&D emerged as a widely recognised industrial force. The success of leading firms in industries such as chemicals, electronics and pharma-ceuticals in exploiting new discoveries for rapid growth in revenues and profits, based on technical developments, generated wide interest in R&D in firms in the USA, Europe and among emerging Japanese firms. The technical virtuosity and spectacular nature of some of the new products blinded too many observers to the practical problem-solving nature of most successful R&D efforts. Businessmen, naive about technology, hoped to 'buy' science and emulate the success of a

DuPont or an old ICI, and aggressive, sometimes arrogant, directors of new, rapidly expanding R&D functions – most without the slightest experience in business – demanded independence and isolation to pursue their ideas. In this sort of unplanned development lie the origins of the transactional gaps between business and research which were the origins of disappointments with R&D in industry in the 1970s and 80s.

John F Magee,[14] then Chairman of the Board of Arthur D Little Inc., makes certain observations in his foreword, which, when compared to real-life experience in industrial R&D laboratories, needs to be questioned seriously. For example, Magee states that executive leadership has come up through the marketing or finance function in which training has not required scientific literacy. He goes on to assert that even today there is a widespread doubt among many scientists and engineers that formal business education can have any useful relevance to their work. Both these views may have had some validity in the 1960s but do not reflect contemporary reality primarily because no sphere of business activity has remained untouched by one or more advanced technological developments. While many business schools have not been able to keep up with rapid technological changes, most successful business leaders as well as engineers and scientists in industry have been forced to metamorphose in order to face the increasingly complex demands of the marketplace. There has been, as a consequence, a growing tendency to weave various specialisms, including R&D, into the corporate fabric in order to achieve business goals.

Magee's second observation is derived from the legitimate preoccupation of management based on measurement (what cannot be measured does not happen!). He argues that the R&D function, however, has characteristically resisted the pressure to make it accountable, because the results most of the time cannot be measured in business terms. It is one of the reasons, he claims, why other functions in business resent the R&D resistance to being held accountable on comparable terms. As I argue throughout my book, for a number of reasons Magee's comments about R&D attitudes are being severely challenged in major firms and in most large corporations. It is now more the rule that management of R&D is subjected to the same disciplines of business accountability. Indeed, many scientists in industry express the fear that such managerial discipline imposed on scientists may severely retard creativity. However, there is now a growing body of evidence which suggests that it is only through the discipline of accountability that some of the most creative scientific discoveries in industries have been turned into big commercial successes. It is also beginning to be gradually accepted that under conditions of so-called 'scientific freedom' and isolation, creative ideas and concepts become diffused and, in many instances, can lead to utter chaos.

The third issue Magee seems to espouse is to consider product and process development as linear activities, that is, as moving in sequence from research to development to engineering to manufacture to sales. The fallacy and failure rate of this linear model of business management is now widely acknowledged and stands discredited. The linear model can be traced to outdated organisational structures and archaic lines of command and control. The radical transformation to flatter organisation structures and formal management processes in teams has been forced by the rising rate of obsolescence of new innovations, the IT revolution and the advances in knowledge management.

The so-called 'first generation' R&D management, which was driven by intuition and act of faith, failed because it depended on allocation of funds to the R&D department with the hope that some good might have emerged. In the 'second generation' process described in the book,[14] R&D was progressively subjected to more rigorous financial rates of return discipline. While this had its virtues, it tended to be overdone to a point which minimised risk taking to a level which also reduced rewards to disproportionately low levels. Roussel *et al.*'s description of the 'third generation' R&D management lists four reasons for the emergence of this methodology. These are:

■ Many corporate leaders have moved beyond the financially driven planning culture of the 1970s.

■ The success of entrepreneurial high technology companies has excited interest in the potential of technology to build company value.

■ More and more industry leaders are seen to give high priority to technology management.

■ Finally, quality and manufacturing competence are seen to be important competitive drivers.

These, then, were some of the factors which triggered the desire to manage R&D in a way that became congruent with business strategy. At the heart of many of the arguments which I make in other chapters of this book, and which some may erroneously dub the 'fourth generation' model, is the realisation that there is a gap between what was clearly seen as desirable as commitment to science and technology, and the difficulties in building these into day-to-day business operations. The gap or disjunction has continued until now to defy logical and dependable managerial processes.

The model for the 'third generation R&D' was meant to provide practical guidance on how to create an environment in which the 'right' R&D is done and which R&D is done correctly to support corporate success. This argument, unfortunately, ignores the influence of complex external factors such as creating and managing academic networks, the differences in consumers and other conditions in different markets around the world and, above all, the critical role of human factors which ultimately determine the degree of integration of R&D into the heartland of corporate operations.

The second weakness in the 'third generation' formula is the recommendation of a generalised hypothesis which is supposed to be used, with necessary variations, at a firm level. While Roussel *et al.* have drawn extensively from the rich experiences of '1,500 ADL consultants who have worked in most major industries throughout the developed and developing world', it is interesting to note that no specific reference is made to the first-hand experiences of successful R&D managers in industry.

Roussel *et al.*'s book which was published in 1991 covered the previous decade in which there was fairly widespread disenchantment in industry with the promise and performance of science. This is reflected in their opening remarks:

> R&D organisations were rarely integrated spiritually or strategically as full and equal partners in the business enterprises whose prosperity they were intended to serve.

This would be a severe indictment of business leaders if this were universally true. The fact remains that right through the 1980s many successful companies had dynamic and productive R&D departments well grafted into the heart of the business, while there were others which had failed to achieve this and suffered adverse consequences as a result. The main reason for some of the disenchantment of the 1980s can be traced to the communication gap between business and research, which becomes even more glaring during business downturn, as was the case in several sectors in the 1980s. No wonder they go on to make the observation:

> we kept wondering why we rarely saw a simple integrated plan in whose creation R&D played a vital role and of which R&D was an inseparable part.

Case studies would have surely exposed at least some of the missing links which have their origins in the history of managerial attitudes and of other unexplored human factors, which then become the black holes in the business galaxy. They conclude:

> that there are common causes, that certain management, R&D planning and operational principles seem universally applicable for superior return from investment in R&D... at the *core* of these principles is the integration of R&D into *partnership* with the corporation and its business.

This otherwise extremely pertinent observation falls short by not probing into the organic nature of such *partnerships*, their sustainability and their creativity potential. It must, however, be acknowledged that Roussel *et al.* did an outstanding job in describing certain important milestones in the evolution of industrial R&D and which, no doubt, provided rich material for further explorations.

Another major focus of Roussel *et al.*'s book is on the strategic deployment of R&D spending. A strong case is made that the business manager should be actively involved with his R&D colleagues in deciding the plans for the R&D budget. This is eminently sensible and no one would disagree with this proposition. But the proposition fails to recognise that management of science and research projects has some unique features other than funding, many of which are at the root of a businessman's disenchantment with industrial R&D. Thus, while elaborate R&D programmes may be prepared by business managers and R&D staff working in harmony, frequently these plans fail to deliver the desired results. In a majority of instances, such failures can be traced to serious disjunctions in the linkage between R&D and the marketplace. In support of their proposition of joint working between business and R&D, Roussel *et al.* refer to quotations from three well-known personalities, all of whom indirectly allude to the all-important human factor. Thus Lowell Steele,[16,17] former Director of Strategic Planning for General Electric, asks:

> How can the Japanese move so fast in introducing new products and responding to market dynamics?

The answer clearly does not lie in access to or use of more advanced technology, because the United States still equals or leads the world in almost every field. *The answer lies in management.* Peter Drucker[18] reinforced the same point in a Harvard Business Review article:

> The one great economic power to emerge in this century – Japan – has not been a technological pioneer in any area. Its ascendancy rests squarely on *leadership in management* [my emphasis].

And Akio Morita[19] of Sony, states:

> Technological management will be the key to success for companies anywhere in the world in the coming years. We are quite advanced in it already. At Sony, we have a monthly R&D meeting *attended by all top executives* and heads of divisions.

In companies where various elements of scientific research, technical development, engineering, manufacturing and marketing work more or less in blissful isolation, poor management becomes quickly evident through business underperformance. Today, there would be rare instances where a business leaves its R&D department more or less alone with the expectation that some spectacular discoveries will emerge to take the marketplace by storm and change the fortunes of the company. However, in the 1950s and 60s this sort of thinking was not that uncommon. The academic community carefully fostered the idea that 'scientists should be left alone to innovate creativity'. Particularly in the USA, defence R&D and NASA fostered the high cost and high rate of the discovery pathway. Thus emerged an industrial approach to R&D which came to be known as 'the strategy of hope'. This was highlighted by Gary Hamel and C K Prahalad,[20] in their *Harvard Business Review* article, which described the Silicon Valley approach to innovation:

Put a few bright people in a dark room, pour in money, and hope.

Considering that industrial civilian R&D was just reviving after the war and costs, in today's terms, were reasonably modest, while one can be over-critical in hindsight, some of the greatest discoveries of this century emerged from such confused beginnings. That such a management approach has outlived its utility is now broadly acknowledged. It is now widely accepted that investment in both academic and industrial R&D will rapidly overtake the import of technology or application of second-hand knowledge for import substitution particularly in newly emerging economies. Newly developing countries can learn some valuable lessons from the experiences of the well-developed economies in planning investments in industrial R&D as well as its management.

The disjunction between corporate goals and the R&D management of the 1950s and 60s has been sought to be mended by better and better management of objectives and the resources with which to achieve them. Both the second and the third generation management of industrial R&D sought greater involvement of business managers as a fundamental requirement. The *general desire* to deliver competitive advantages in business through R&D has been replaced by a *compulsion* to do so today. It is this compulsion which defines the emergence of business-driven R&D as a core corporate objective. As I describe elsewhere in the book, the third generation process differs from current practices by the latter being holistic in terms of encompassing the external world of science and technology, on the one hand, and coupling it with a deep understanding of the dynamics of consumer needs, on the other. In other words, while the third generation process represents a step in the right direction, it remains incomplete as far as deriving maximum advantage from industrial R&D by not putting it alongside all other business processes.

Roussel *et al.* (1991, p. 8) underline the weakness of the third generation process thus:

The difference between the R&D management of the 1930s and today's third generation R&D management is discernible not in the attitudes or activities of the R&D manager but the environment in which he operates.

This argument is fundamentally flawed because both the speed of change in science and the complexity of business have no resemblance to conditions in the 1930s. That today, the skills and competencies required to manage business successfully and consistently, would be several degrees higher is natural. To aver that such changes have limited influence in the way we work and interact would be grossly understating the case. Their other observation, that people were more co-operative and had a natural affinity to work together in creative pursuits in the 1930s compared to present times, is another over-simplification compared to the realities of today's workplace.

There are some myths which keep cropping up with regularity in discussions on managing industrial R&D. One myth is that since most corporate senior managers and directors emerge from the finance and marketing streams, the communication gap with scientists and engineers is impossible to bridge. The danger of this argument is that it appears to be superficially convincing. But it grossly underestimates the intelligence, competence, curiosity and the natural drive which distinguishes successful business managers, and overstates the complexity of science and engineering. In most instances, where business leaders avoid interaction with R&D, such avoidance can be traced to a subconscious 'x' factor attributable to R&D, and which business setbacks are easily foisted upon. Similarly, scientists and engineers who use complexity as an excuse to avoid intimate dialogue and interactions with their business colleagues are frequently found to be wanting in their own disciplines and find the isolation a protection from their lack of competence being exposed.

Another myth which reappears with regular frequency is that too much accountability and management by business process dampens creativity. This is a very old myth perpetuated by generation after generation of scientists to explain their need to remain in ivory towers, thus insulating their minds and thoughts from the day-to-day vagaries of society. Until not so long ago, scientists were indeed held in some awe by the general public and there was a consensus in society that practitioners of science had to be left alone and undisturbed to pursue creativity. Since science has played such a spectacular role in the economic and evolutionary advances of human society, some of the reverence was quite natural and understandable. However, due to a number of factors the traditionally superior status of scientists in society now stands severely challenged. While there are a number of factors which have changed society's attitude towards scientists, the more salient ones are worth recalling. Scientists by nature and training tend to be more optimistic compared to the general population. They therefore frequently seem to promise more than they are able to deliver. The gap between promise and delivery now tends to be exaggerated by overexposure of setbacks and failures in the media and across the global information network. The growth of problems which affect the majority of people, such as the environment, population, hunger, modern diseases and so on, tends to be blamed, at least in part, on the inability of science to deal effectively with such problems. Whether this is correct or otherwise, as a view, is another matter. Similarly, in industry when the fortunes of a corporation receive a serious setback, it is not unusual to find the chief executive attributing it to the failure of the scientists and engineers to deliver on their promise. The issue is extremely well articulated by Jerome Wiesner,[21] Institute Professor Emeritus and the former President of MIT, as follows:

> The major problem in both cases (the US steel and automotive industries) was at the top. These two industries were plagued by leaders who lacked a vision of continued greatness for their companies or any appreciation of what science and technology could do for them.

The latest book on R&D in industry (1998) has been written by J V Buckley[15]. Buckley is a consultant with PA Consulting Group. In a reasonably lucid account, he describes some traditional issues such as the distinction between 'research' and 'development', the role of CEOs and senior managers to set up the R&D agenda, the management of innovation and its delivery process. Buckley has buttressed his arguments by interesting case studies, of which one pertaining to General Motors is particularly interesting. I will refer to it in due course.

In his introduction, Buckley declares he is 'not a technologist'. He worked in British Telecommunications as a network specialist, and his description of both the conduct of research and business indeed reflects the views of a generalist. If one has not undergone the discipline, the rigour and the eventual enrichment of the mind by being exposed to fundamental scientific enquiry, which is amply provided especially in American and European universities, it is virtually impossible to comprehend what original scientific exploration and research is all about. It is, to a degree, similar to not having experience of managing a business, competing in the marketplace, making profits and creating shareholder value and solely depending on generalised case studies to seek solutions to business problems.

Thus Buckley's portrayal of scientists and technologists as being disconnected from the business process is as outdated as his claim that 'most senior managers do not have a scientific and engineering background', thereby implying that they are somewhat at the mercy of the R&D specialists even in this day and age. The days when business managers felt intimidated by technologists are long past. Today, it would indeed be rare where a CEO or a business manager does not have a remarkably strong grasp of technological developments at least in their own core business areas. The days when scientists and technologists bedazzled administrators or business managers by abstract scientific jargon and promises shrouded in complexity have also passed. It is now widely accepted that no area of science or technology is so complex that it cannot be explained in a layperson's terms. On the contrary, topics which tend to get obfuscated by jargon are invariably looked upon with suspicion precisely because of lack of clarity. The demystification of science is now well advanced and nothing is likely to reverse this trend.

The other point made by Buckley (1998, p. 4) and which is bound to be contentious is that

> Research is the domain of academia and no industrial organisation should be undertaking this work.

He goes on to proclaim that 'Essentially, any "investment" in academic research should be regarded as dead money' since the odds on its delivering any returns to the business may be considered the same as those of winning a national lottery. As anyone with even a rudimentary understanding of scientific research and R&D management will be aware, nothing could be further from reality. A degree of firm-level core competency in basic scientific research is absolutely a prerequisite for undertaking even modestly productive industrial R&D. Otherwise most industries would have gladly saved the money allocated to in-house basic research. It is certainly not a supply-chain issue as implied by Buckley in the statement 'it is an activity more appropriately contracted out to Universities, technology institutes or contract research organisations'.

Regarding development, Buckley has this to say:

If a company has a development group that is applying scientific, engineering or technological knowledge in a systematic way to improve
performance, it can start thinking about going for growth and
increasing shareholder value.

What remains unexplained is how a firm foregathers such talent and is
able to provide it with the resources to update their knowledge
continuously, given the explosion in the advances in practically all
disciplines of science.

Buckley's third fallacy is contained in the statement that 'marketers
and technologists seldom mix well'. Nothing of course can be further
from reality in any modern and successful business. It is well known
that most companies aim to impart the latest technology into their
products and services, based entirely on superior market knowledge
and marketing leadership. This would not be possible if scientists and
marketers did not work in cohesive harmony.

Buckley's exhortation to CEOs and senior managers to beware of
R&D personnel is likely to make the latter more defensive and unproductive, as has been the experience of most companies who have
sought to 'control' R&D and its costs. Truly competent managers of
R&D do not use risks and uncertainties inherent in scientific research
with which to exercise their power in a company. These concepts are
so outdated that to use them to seek change as we approach a new
millennium is indeed beguiling.

The argument that all the S&T (science and technology) needed
by a firm cannot be sustained at the firm level because of the rapid
change in both S&T as well as the marketplace, while factually
correct, is distorted by cost arguments and making a case for
outsourcing. And even in this case, the sheer complexity of creating
and managing productive external scientific networks and partnerships is grossly underestimated. In the same vein, Buckley states that
'research is arguably the most costly, most complex and least
productive industrial activity that any firm can get involved in' and
that 'essentially, the link between research and shareholder is often
weak or non-existent'. Such a conclusion can only be arrived at in
the absence of real-life experience. Buckley (1998, p. 23) stands
exposed when he claims that:

whereas research explores basic science, has no obvious end-product or process, consumes large amounts of investments, and is arguably the most costly, most complex and least productive industrial activity, development is the exploitation of technology created elsewhere.

Buckley's observations are even more surprising when placed next to the brief but lucid case study of General Motors quoted halfway through his text. The efforts of Ken Baker, the General Motors' R&D Director, to transform R&D into a business-driven process, highlighting the importance of scientific research and technology development, and woven into the rest of the General Motors business process, should have alerted Buckley to the realities of the role of modern R&D in industry. Although in a subsequent account of innovation and its management, Buckley does refer to interdisciplinary project teams and project ownership by business managers, this exhortation stands in stark contradiction with the rest of the text. Unfortunately, this latest book on industrial R&D has also been written by a non-practitioner and suffers from all the disadvantages without exploring the complexities of R&D as a vital wealth-creating activity.

In contrast to these two recent books on R&D in industry, two other recent articles provide very refreshing and contemporary accounts. One of these is an excellent article in *The Economist* [22] under the title 'The Rebirth of IBM'. The article observes that, before it was almost destroyed by the personal computing revolution it helped start, IBM was a model, not just for its own industry, but for the rest of corporate America. Now, after five years of the leadership of Lou Gerstner, it believes it can play that role again. How did Mr Gerstner do it? And can such a broad-based technology firm ever compete with its more specialised rivals? Mr Gerstner had run American Express during a period when information technology had become increasingly important. American Express was building a giant network moving data all over the world. Mr Gerstner knew that IBM had some first-class people and great technology. But as one of those customers, Mr Gerstner had found IBM increasingly out of touch with his needs. As one IBM researcher who has been quoted in *The Economist* [22] article states:

in those days we just threw the technology over the wall to see who would pick it up. Quite often IBM only got interested when another company went off with it.

Mr Gerstner was convinced that IBM's size and scope, instead of being a disadvantage, made it uniquely able to provide what he was convinced customers were looking for – SOLUTIONS.

IBM was posting big losses. It would have been easy to have taken an axe to IBM's $6 billion-a-year R&D budget. In particular, the research division, with its love for esoteric long-term projects that never saw the light of day and its record of producing winning ideas for competitors, must have looked ripe for the chop. But Mr Gerstner was so impressed by what he saw on his first visit to the Watson research centre that he stayed his hand. Budgets were pruned but long-term research continued. Mr Gerstner has, however, pushed the researchers to spend more time working on solutions with real customers. Nearly one-third of IBM's research is now conducted with customers through a process known as 'first of its kind'. An example is a project with Monsanto to map the genetic structure of plant and human diseases using computing techniques that defeated world chess champion Gary Kasparov.

Regaining leadership is Mr Gerstner's goal of his second five years with IBM. When asked what that means he says, 'Our customers will tell us if we have achieved it. That's the only definition of leadership that matters.'

Finally, in their forthcoming book Downes and Mui[23] make the following profound observation:

> Traditionally, strategy has come from the top of the company with technology being one of its constituent parts. But in more and more cases technology is the strategy. What is more, it comes from below: from customers and those in the company closest to them. When technology changes from being a component in the business to the business itself, the way to find out is when it is no longer possible to tell where the business stops and the technology begins.

3 Knowledge and its Management

Introduction

No world-class enterprise will be able to grow and thrive if it is not being driven by a constantly updated pool of knowledge. Such corporations are marked by their business leaders' ability to define a business vision for the firm which encompasses deep knowledge of the short, medium and longer term aspects of global, competitive and consumer elements. Such knowledge-based business vision provides a starting point to define specific business goals and objectives. Inevitably, such a knowledge-driven process generates innumerable opportunities and forces a business to choose priorities. The choice and management of priorities then becomes the joint task of business and R&D managers. While the business managers remain accountable for the performance of the bottom line, in this process the R&D managers' accountability is also clearly defined in measurable terms regarding its impact on the bottom line as well. *This is entirely a modern way of managing knowledge for the creation of wealth.* On its consistent application depends the health and well-being of a firm and, in a larger national context, the comprehension and use of this process can and does change fortunes of societies.

Thus, while R&D is charged with the production of new knowledge, business is required to incorporate such knowledge into goods and services and thus seek competitive advantage. In this paradigm, the definition of the consumer expectations from a firm's goods and services becomes the fundamental driver for the exploration and generation of the knowledge needed to create new products and services.

The fundamental shift in the way knowledge is influencing business-driven R&D is becoming abundantly clear by its close integration with the rest of the firm. It is the customer and the marketplace which define the needs for goods and services. The business managers' role is to comprehend and translate such expressed, and frequently unexpressed needs, in terms of business opportunities and priorities. Business managers and R&D managers then have to work jointly to transform such opportunities and priorities into successful marketable products, to the advantage of the firm and its stakeholders.

In any dynamic and leading-edge firm, business opportunities will always tend to exceed the resources available to it. This situation becomes much more acute when business and R&D managers are faced with the choice of priority projects. Attractive and alternative marketing and R&D opportunities always exceed the resources available in a firm. The temptation, both in the business and even more so in R&D, is to stretch resources to undertake more projects than can be effectively managed. The choice of a manageable number of priorities, and the assessment of risks and rewards, probably are the most important defining steps which distinguish a consistently successful corporation. In more philosophical terms *less is more* probably provides an ideal holistic definition of such management style and practice.

Knowledge, its generation, management and application in a business are thus the primary links between R&D and the marketplace. It is therefore worth exploring some contemporary issues related to knowledge and its impact on business-driven R&D.

Background

Knowledge has emerged as the prime driving force in world business and commerce. While one might argue that this may have always been so since the dawn of civilisation and even more explicitly after the industrial revolution, as the narrative to follow will try and describe, there has occurred a more radical transformation in the production and application of knowledge in the past quarter century or so. This new knowledge revolution has been primarily driven by advances in *Information Technology* and *Global Telephony*. While the USA has been the fountainhead of all modern developments in the production and use of knowledge, the Netherlands was probably the first country officially to accord knowledge a national priority. The Netherlands declared in the mid-1990s that the production and application of knowledge will be the prime force for economic development in the emerging world order. Since then, most economically advanced countries now agree that *competitive advantage can only be derived by the generation and management of knowledge as a surrogate to trade and services*. It is probable that many of the developing economies will eventually recognise this paradigm. They will need to in order to reinforce national core competencies, at the firm level, in different sectors such as education and R&D, as well as in defining national policies and strategy.

While knowledge is fast becoming the dominant factor in determining global terms of trade, its impact on education, academic R&D and R&D in industry is probably more far reaching and visibly more prominent than in any other sector. It is this fact which has prompted me to describe the relationship between knowledge, education and R&D, as well as certain related aspects of social developments. Many of the subsequent chapters will frequently refer back to different aspects of modern knowledge development, described in this chapter.

Two recent seminal texts[24,25] on the subject of knowledge provide the backdrop for the narrative that follows. While Nonaka and Takeuchi[24] have tried to explain how and why Japanese companies exploit knowledge differently (and, according to the authors, better!) compared to their counterparts in the West, Gibbons *et al.* [25] describe the various elements of knowledge from a more universal perspective.

A modern concept of knowledge

The shift in the nature of production and use of knowledge has been occurring for quite a while. However, it is more recently, and primarily driven by advances in IT, that the profound impact of this shift is being felt in academia and industry, as well as at the national level (in politics for example), and particularly in the advanced economies. The comprehension of such developments in the rest of the nations of the world has been, until now, extremely superficial. Since knowledge management and wealth creation are interrelated, a growing knowledge gap between the so-called rich and poor countries is likely to widen further the disparities and tensions around the world. Since knowledge is becoming the main differentiator in civil societies, the relative competencies and competitiveness of nations are facing a paradigm shift. The collapse of the economies of southern Latin America in the early 1980s and the meltdown of the 'tiger' economies of Asia in 1997/98 can, at least in part, be traced to limits to knowledge production and management competencies in many of these countries. The Japanese meltdown is somewhat exceptional in itself, but as will be described later on, may be traced to some of the Japanese characteristics described by Nonaka and Takeuchi.[24]

Probably the most visible impact in terms of transformation in the way knowledge is dealt with can be seen in the USA and countries of Western Europe. The conflict between the traditionalists and modernists, even in these countries, has not yet been fully resolved. This is probably most visible in the academic world where the nostalgia for the warmth and comfort of ivory towers has not disappeared altogether, although the towers are turning distinctly colder.

The former Soviet Union and China provide some unusual and unique lessons with regard to the use and abuse of knowledge. During the cold war years, it was generally acknowledged that in the Soviet Union, defence-related R&D was comparable to that of the West. As a matter of fact the Soviets were first to place a satellite in outer space as well as launch the first manned spacecraft. Yet, after the cold war ended and the Soviet Union disintegrated, so did its massive knowledge organisations, built up since World War II. The complete isolation of the civilian from the defence sector created unbridgeable barriers in Russia and its plans for economic revival. This is a lesson other nations need to heed as well.

As the Russian example demonstrates, the generally held belief that enormous sums spent on defence R&D will somehow impart a multiplier impact on civilian R&D remains more or less unsubstantiated,[26] while China provides a different but no less interesting example. During the great Chinese Cultural Revolution there were widespread campaigns mounted against schools, universities, academics and intellectuals across China as root sources of revisionist ideologies. As a consequence, during this period lasting a number of years, millions of Chinese were deprived of primary, secondary and university education. Civilian R&D ground to a standstill. How much of the aftermath of this failed revolution spurred China to open its economy to Western and Japanese technology and investment starting in 1978 is worth investigating further. Unlike Russia, China realised that the loss of its civilian knowledge pool following the cultural revolution could not be rebuilt even with the help of its powerful military establishment, and that its knowledge gap could only be bridged by importing technology from advanced nations.

From these two important and contemporary examples, it may be apparent that knowledge, education, R&D and wealth creation are not only intimately linked, but people and nations who master this value chain help advance the cause of civil society, while those who are unable to cope, or decide to follow another model, tend to slide into regressive underdevelopment.

As will be discussed in due course, generation and management of knowledge is becoming so complex, and its impact on societies growing so rapidly, that collaboration between the sources and users of knowledge is acquiring unprecedented importance. For example, the current push to create economically sustainable 'clean' technologies is about more than just economic benefit. It is also about stabilising collapsing ecological systems and the health and well-being of populations, as well as generating commercial gains from making the world a better place to live in.

Knowledge, research and education

There has been unprecedented growth in the development of mass higher education in the industrialised countries after World War II. This has permanently changed the attitude towards work in every stratum of society and has been the principal driving force for increase in innovations in traditional industries as well as the explosive growth of service industries. These developments have naturally influenced the traditional ways of pursuing scientific and technological research. Research is still considered an elite activity in spite of a large number of people involved in teams trying to solve problem clusters in well-defined projects. As mentioned elsewhere, research funding and programmes are also under greater public and government scrutiny and accountability. In spite of the desire to hold on to the conditions and environment of an earlier era, researchers and research establishments are inexorably getting involved in working relationships with people in different spheres and typically include business people, patent lawyers, innovation managers and others located outside the university.

In the wake of these developments a host of new institutional arrangements are also emerging linking government, industry, universities and private consultancy groups in new and productive ways. To a noticeable extent, traditional university-restricted research is giving way to new collaborative networks with other institutions and industry, driven by traditional curiosity drive, but coupled, in most instances, by the wealth creation motive. The Framework R&D programme of the European Union represents a massive geographical initiative of such a kind. Its sole purpose is to bring together, via funding mechanisms, clusters of small, medium and large enterprises, along with appropriate research institutes and university departments, to work on megascientific problems, the fruits of whose solutions are then supposed to be divided in some preordained manner. While this initiative has raised the critical resource and intellectual mass for key areas of research in Europe, the cost benefit of such efforts and their economic value creation remains somewhat vague. Notwithstanding such uncertainties, the commitment to collaborative inter- and trans-disciplinary research has increased all across the European community and represents a major cultural shift from the traditional ways and attitudes of scientists and technologists. In addition, a very well-conceived *human mobility programme* has catalysed the movement of budding scientists into laboratories all across Europe, solely on the basis of their core competency and the programme needs in different geographical locations. The European Union DGXII has also pioneered the development of the concept of *demonstrator projects* with the sole objective of enabling small and medium enterprises to afford the risk involved in developing and commercialising new technologies. While the Framework initiative of the European Union has taken full advantage of the emerging collaborative formations, this has not yet been wholeheartedly embraced by parts of the academic communities in different European countries. Many academics participate in programmes primarily because the Framework has become a valuable funding source. But gradually and perceptibly the realisation has begun to dawn, even in tradition-bound academic communities, that collaborative scientific research may be the most effective way of solving megascientific problems, and that wealth creation from R&D is the legitimate expectation of the rest of society.

At the national level, the LINK and Foresight programmes in the UK are similar inter- and trans-disciplinary efforts to raise the competitiveness of the country, domestically as well as in exports, to create employment and generate wealth.[27] In both these initiatives, that is, Framework and LINK, the biggest unresolved issue is that of the management of mega projects. There are as yet no formal institutional mechanisms to train managers and equip them professionally to manage large R&D projects and multiparty, multidisciplinary collaborative programmes. Currently such programmes tend to be co-ordinated by traditional management consultants. While most of them provide adequate co-ordination and supervisory service, the vital elements of extracting synergies and exploring potential value generators tend to be missing. Even in the USA, where large-scale state and industry sponsored collaborative R&D began 10–15 years before Europe, most of the business schools have tended to skirt the whole area of providing formal training in R&D management. *For this state of affairs both the business schools as well as the R&D community are responsible in equal measure.*

Certain aspects in the changing attitude to the traditional ways of thinking and working can be traced to the evolution in education and its ready availability to the masses. For example, the explosive growth of primary, secondary and higher education has had the highest impact in the USA and Europe and explains, at least in part, the economic advances in these nations. Japan is somewhat unique although its investment in education is no less impressive. The impact of investment in education in the emerging economies remains less well understood. For example, what is described as the 1997/98 melt-down in the Tiger economies in East Asia can be, at least partly, traced to their inability to generate a sufficient number of knowledge workers. And as mentioned earlier, during Mao's great Cultural Revolution, most educational institutions and those engaged in higher education and research were either destroyed or closed down for several years. Although China today has a high literacy rate, several millions of Chinese were deprived of formal education during the Cultural Revolution. The impact of the Cultural Revolution on China's economic development remains unexplored. India has the largest number of illiterate people in the world due to gross under-investment in education and failure of literacy initiatives at the national level. This has now been recognised as one of the major reasons for India's poor economic development, although at times this tends to be wrongly overshadowed by India's growing importance as a software centre. Similar conditions of poor investment in education prevail in southern Latin America, Africa and Eastern Europe.

The impact of mass higher education in the economic transformation of the USA, Western Europe and Japan is now considered as the most profound factor in the explosive growth of small service and high technology industries, generating unprecedented opportunities for knowledge workers. Among the most significant efforts of mass higher education, of special significance for the production and distribution of knowledge is the great increase in the market for continuous education, and thus of the emergence of a learning society, one in which life-long study as well as training and retraining are possible and now taken for granted by large segments of the population. The readiness to learn greatly increases the capacity of a working population to respond to rapid technological change and drives innovation, competitiveness as well as new employment generation or renewal. In such an emerging culture of learning, it teaches people not to become too closely devoted to one occupation or a single set of skills. The only skill that does not become obsolete is the skill of learning new skills.

The trend noticed in mass higher education naturally has a profound influence on the training of scientists and conduct of scientific research. This is the basis of the emergence of new forms of research in the USA and EU which require close working relationships between people located in different institutions, not all of whom need be scientists. Thus there are formally designed interactions of university-based researchers with business people, venture capitalists, patent lawyers, production engineers, as well as research engineers and scientists located outside the university. This invariably involves shared use of academic and industrial facilities. Under these conditions, technology, is more likely to be trans-disciplinary, and to be carried out by people who are able to rise above disciplinary and institutional loyalties.

These and similar changes and transformations are advancing so rapidly that their impact on traditional institutions and attitudes has just begun to be understood. Thus traditional funding from central government or non-profit foundations is increasingly being supplemented or at least partly being replaced by the firms, industries and social lobbies directly involved.

The conduct of research in the context of wealth creation is primarily derived from its distributed nature, which means that contemporary science can no longer remain within the confines of university departments or academic centres. This is leading to the emergence of a host of new institutional arrangements linking government, industry, universities and private consultancy groups, as described earlier, as an illustration, in the EU Framework initiative.

The tradition of academic independence is deemed by many, especially in Europe, to be threatened by encroachment of industry driven by its commercial goals. But it is equally becoming clear that this type of research formation and collaboration is not only increasing but is being compelled by rising research costs, and the need to raise the effectiveness of knowledge-driven competitiveness. As a matter of fact, academic independence and objectivity are qualities which, if anything, are even more critical for industrial collaborations to be productive and dependable. Academic independence is thus strengthened by the tacit acknowledgement of its objectivity and at the same time made transparent and accountable, unlike in earlier times.

Another fear expressed, fairly widely, is that such collaborative formations may shift the character of academic research and training, making it less and less curiosity driven and more and more aimed towards solving specific problems of defined purpose. Any reasonable scientist can immediately detect the utter fallacy in this argument because any scientific enquiry, either defined or undefined, is fundamentally 'curiosity driven' because that indeed is the nature of scientific research. While the luxury of either undefined or amorphous curiosity indeed is being questioned more and more, there is no evidence to suggest that this has affected funding of genuine research in fields ranging from particle physics to a variety of combinatorial sciences.

From the perspective of the overall research scenario, the need for external funding encourages professors, and hence universities, to be responsive to societal demands. Academic departments, as a consequence, have to be much more flexible, which enables research groups to shift research interests and to move quickly into new exciting areas. From the perspective of industry, this is a valuable development and the reason why universities are seen as the primary source of competence in basic research, and complementary to different strengths of industry.

Research in industry, even if physical conditions may be better than most university laboratories, presents a totally different set of scientific and managerial problems (which are described in a separate chapter). Briefly, a balance has to be maintained between basic research, technology programmes and product and process innovations. Given the rapid advances in every discipline of science and engineering, it is no longer possible for any individual firm, no matter what its size and financial resources, to sustain a critical mass in basic research within its physical premises. Happily, many leading academics and universities are well aware of emerging needs of basic research in industry and consider them to be favourable factors in creating lasting partnerships with individual firms, both for the benefit of the firm and to sustain their own academic excellence and creativity. Thus, in contrast to multipartner, state-sponsored collaborative research, dedicated partnership research programmes tend to be much more productive and longer lasting, provided, of course, they are managed competently and fairly. In such partnerships, over a period of time, the distinction between basic and goal-orientated research becomes blurred and academic freedom acquires a more contemporary and socially acceptable status.

What has been described until now signals an evolutionary development consisting of radical transformation in the philosophy, organisation structures and cultures of even some of the oldest and most venerable universities. The USA pioneered the process, in the early part of this century, by establishing the land-grant colleges to drive up agricultural productivity and improve farm economies. Over a period, and especially after World War II, this philosophy of wealth-creating partnership spread to other activities in the USA, especially to manufacturing and service industries. The collaboration philosophy has escalated in the last 10–15 years by the spread of venture capitalism, which has given a whole new meaning to risk taking and entrepreneurship. The EU is trying to draw heavily from the successful American experience, although both industry and academia in Europe still have some way to go to derive the fullest advantages in order to become a knowledge-driven society. Historically, Japan was extremely reluctant to bring academia and industry together in a collaborative mode. Because of such local attitudes and obstacles, many Japanese firms sought alternatives to establish collaborative partnerships with universities in the USA and Europe. Unfortunately, the productivity and effectiveness of such cross-geographical arrangements in wealth creation remain somewhat obscure. Most other countries have yet to become aware of such massive transformations taking place in relationships in the academic, industrial and social spheres, and how such relationships are providing impetus to the harnessing and exploitation of knowledge with which to generate wealth and provide social good.

The much-maligned multinational corporations (MNCs) are among the pioneers in spreading the concept of knowledge management in different geographical locations almost as an economic compulsion demanded by their core investments. Prior to making new investments, MNCs generally assess certain preconditions which are necessary for the development of knowledge-generating links to a local market. One such precondition is the existence of a good educational infrastructure in a market and a second, which to an extent follows, is the availability of skilled manpower required to manage new knowledge networks. However, as a result of the rapid globalisation of business and commerce, MNCs, with a few exceptions, are now finding it more difficult to sustain meaningful knowledge bases in dispersed geographical territories. There are probably two reasons for such a state of affairs. First, many MNCs are engaged in changing to new ways of managing knowledge in their own headquarters and thus do not have enough resources to create and sustain networks in the emerging markets. Second, at least some MNCs are discovering that certain cultural and financial hurdles to exploiting modern knowledge networks in alien surroundings can be substantial, for example, as some of the Japanese MNCs are discovering after making large investments in American and European universities.

In conclusion of this section, it may be stated that while the systems and methodologies to generate and manage knowledge were pioneered in the USA, and represent the engine of America's growth and prosperity, the massification of education in Europe, especially since the war, is beginning to enable the countries of the European Union to match the American challenge. Japan, on the other hand, has demonstrated certain unique strengths as well as vulnerabilities, some of which at least can be traced to its social and cultural roots. The failure of the socialist economies can be traced, at least in part, to the inadequacies in the way knowledge was generated and managed, while limitations in knowledge management led to restricting growth in most other developing and underdeveloped economies. The modern MNCs are probably the most effective catalysts in establishing and managing global knowledge networks dedicated to wealth creation.

Some trends in the evolution of knowledge

Researchers tend to classify technological knowledge into two – *codified* and *tacit* components. While *codified* knowledge, as it implies, can be stored and retrieved when needed, *tacit* knowledge is defined as 'residing in the heads' of specialists. At the firm level, while codified knowledge can be protected as intellectual property, *tacit* knowledge is usually in the form of skills and competencies of specialist employees. Thus there are both knowledge elements as well as human factors which determine the effectiveness of interdisciplinary and trans-disciplinary exploitation of a knowledge pool. It is therefore easy to see that firms which are able to pool and exploit such diverse elements deliberately, tend to win and lead. Sometimes the outcome of such a process is called 'creativity'. Dominance depends on creativity, which is a matter of skills, resources and organisation.

The inter- or trans-disciplinary approach in knowledge advancement has been explored in depth by Gibbons *et al.* [25] and their explorations provide a number of interesting insights. The break-up and reordering of traditional scientific disciplines such as mathematics, physics, chemistry and biology has been going on for several decades. As long as the new interdisciplinary activities remained within the physical proximity of the traditional disciplines, they were not only tolerated by academic gurus, but encouraged as symbols of modernisation. Even leading business schools were not able to comprehend fully the emergence of interdisciplinarity as a powerful new business tool. At best, by interfacing with engineering departments and developing joint programmes on technology management and supply chain exploration, business schools considered they were initiating revolutionary changes. Such initiatives, of course, fell far short of what was really needed. The management of R&D, as practised in academia as well as in industry, thus remained more or less outside the focus of virtually all business schools. Industry, with a few exceptions, was more or less unaware of these developments in new knowledge management in the early post war years. Ironically, the real upheaval in inter- and trans-disciplinary reordering of science was initiated by industry itself which saw a whole plethora of exciting business opportunities emerge following the unravelling of the structure of DNA by Watson and Crick and the explosion of the chip-driven growth fuelled by Silicon Valley.

As a consequence of these developments, a whole new way of generating, managing and exploiting knowledge began to emerge. Because the emergence of this new way of working had not been clearly foreseen or visualised and did not quite fit the linear management models of the day, the creation of trans- and intradisciplinary science clusters, which were task or sector specific, evolved more or less by trial and error. The methods of management applied to national tasks, such as the Manhattan Project during the war or in time of national self-doubt, for example, Kennedy's 'man on the moon' target, were rightly considered as both inappropriate and unviable in the civilian sector.

The complexity of the trans- and interdisciplinary management of science disciplines arises from task-specific and continuous linking, delinking and relinking, in specific clustering and configuration of knowledge which is brought together within a time and cost framework. The dynamic, transient and task-specific nature of the process makes it difficult to codify the methodology except in broad terminology, but this very uncertainty creates a new climate of excitement and energy, both among academics and industrial scientists, for further search and exploitation. This is especially so for those who are inclined to step out of the traditional boundaries of their science disciplines.

While many management experts have dwelt at length on subjects such as corporate re-engineering or renewal, the literature on re-engineering industrial R&D or academic re-engineering is very sparse because it remains relatively under-explored (see Chapter 2).

Gibbons *et al.*[25] quite accurately observe that in this trans-disciplinary context, disciplinary boundaries, distinctions between pure and applied research and institutional differences between, say, universities and industry, are becoming less and less relevant. Instead, attention is focused primarily on the problem area, or the hot topic, preference given to collaborative rather than individual performance and excellence judged by ability of individuals to make a sustained contribution in open, flexible types of organisations (for example, teams) in which they may only work temporarily. Nonetheless, a new mode of knowledge production cannot simply force its way onto the institutional stage in any given set-up. It calls for a 'make-break-make' model which entails a totally new and unprecedented set of task-driven interactions between academics and industrial R&D on the one hand, alongside transformation of the R&D business processes which are primarily opportunity as well as threat driven. The only condition which would naturally facilitate the emergence of this new way of working would be its overpowering logic which appeals to all the constituents, as well as its transparency which can raise the veil of traditional distrust among the different constituents. Such transparency also facilitates a degree of social and economic accountability which both academic and industrial scientists have, historically, vehemently resisted as being inimical to creativity. While society readily acknowledges the elitist nature of the practice of scientific research, it no longer feels that the cloak of isolation and mystery is acceptable in these modern times. This again has been facilitated by advances in IT and telecommunication, as a result of which not only are people living in advanced countries better informed, virtually about everything and anything, but such information now readily flows even to remote parts of the less developed world. The more recent incidents of what is popularly called 'mad cow disease' in the UK are generally perceived by the public as an alarming and current example of scientific mismanagement and lack of transparency on the part of the scientific community. Such incidents reinforce the growing distrust of the public with regard to 'expert advice'. Similarly, the inability of scientists and engineers to provide clearer linkages between atmospheric pollution and climate change is being watched with a great deal of apprehension by countries all around the world. The reappearance of old infectious diseases, but with new organisms causing them, and the medical profession's inability to deal with these comprehensively, has added further strain on the credibility of the scientific community. In such a prevalent public mood, even perfectly logical advances made in agricultural genetics are being opposed by organised groups of people in society even though some of these discoveries hold the key to food security and sustainable agriculture of the future. The human genome project, on the other hand, is significantly more profound than either the Manhattan project or even the 'man on the moon' initiative referred to earlier. It is more than likely that we will be able, in a few years from now, permanently to change human health and well-being on this universe. The knowledge of the human gene will spawn a radically different health care and pharmaceutical industry. The quality of life will be profoundly changed for the better and so on and on and on. And yet even in the early phase of the genome project a great controversy has erupted about the use of genetic information by insurance companies to ascertain levels of premiums. Such instances of spectacular discovery as well as heightened distrust keeps growing virtually every day.

These are a few examples which highlight how the explosive growth of new knowledge is creating unlimited interdisciplinary permutations of opportunities in science, demanding novel collaborative endeavours and so on, and thus impacting every segment of our society, while at the same time demanding totally new methods of management, transparency and accountability from the knowledge-creating community.

Thus, while knowledge production within traditional disciplinary structures remains valid, interesting and important, a set of new inter- and intradisciplinary methodologies are growing out of these traditional structures and are now progressing alongside them. Although they are at an early stage of development, some of the practices associated with the new mode of working are beginning to generate pressures for radical change in traditional methods of the state planned and funded scientific research. Not surprisingly, some of the traditional institutions are resistant particularly to those changes which seem to be threatening the very structures and processes which have been created to protect the integrity of scientific discipline.

Some transitional issues

Some of the pressures being generated by the demands for radical changes being imposed by the new knowledge paradigm hinge on what is meant by science and technology. This is to a large extent determined by what scientists and technologists are accustomed to and the ways in which they produce knowledge. Not only do those claiming to produce scientific knowledge have to follow some generally accepted methods, but they also must be trained in the appropriate procedures and techniques of scientific enquiry. To be funded, researchers must formulate the problems on which they want to work in specific ways, recognisable by their peers, and they must be scrupulous in reporting their experiments and results to this community using prescribed modes of communication. Thus traditional structures and norms provide both quality control by peers and social reassurance in the public domain. Many thus argue that knowledge cannot qualify as scientific if it is practised and produced outside its legitimate (traditional) structures. However, this view is now seriously challenged by forces of which some lie outside the academic and scientific domain. For example, at different times in history what constitutes good science has been guided by the ideal of truth and the search for a unitary principle. In the newly emerging reality, the quality of assessing research is twofold. One has to do with the rise and importance of trans- and interdisciplinarity and the criterion of quality has additionally to answer such questions as application and value creation. Because the world has moved along and away from the linear model of discovery, application and exploitation to a stage where discovery and application are becoming almost inseparable, in the majority of instances, the relevant science being produced is specifically to provide solutions to well-defined problems.

Since science and R&D, in principle, can be virtually sourced from anywhere in the world, the role that specialised knowledge has come to play in technological innovation has become a prime force in the growth of inter- and trans-disciplinarity. In such new and unusual heterogeneous configurations, communication and task management have acquired critical importance. Whereas advances in IT keep improving communications as means of extracting value from inter- and trans-disciplinarity, the means of developing managers especially trained to manage and advance large knowledge-generating teams and networks remain grossly neglected (see Chapter 7).

I have earlier, briefly, referred to the issue of accountability of science to society. Globalisation of trade and commerce adds an even greater urgency to this obligation. Traditionally, communication between science and society was essentially one way: scientists were the holders and generators of privileged expert knowledge, while the lay public was meant to be enlightened and educated. But the pressures for account-ability from an increasingly better informed and better educated public have permanently changed this relationship, in two ways. First, in every country there is now much greater pressure to justify public expenditure on science. Second, resource is only one aspect of a much broader social concern with the conduct and goals of scientific research.

There is, as a consequence, an ever growing demand for social as well as financial accountability from the scientific community and its funders. The most sensitive domains so far have centred upon techno-logical risks, notably those connected with nuclear power and other large technical facilities; environmental concerns covering a wide range of topics from oestrogen in the environment to the ozone layer, besides the raging debate on the ethical issues concerning genetic engineering in plants, animals and humans. The historic claims that scientific research does not have any boundaries and is always meant for the advancement of humankind, now has to meet certain legiti-mate questions as to what precisely is meant by 'advancement of humankind' as well as other concerns of a society in which it operates.

Therefore, the manner in which the scientific community now communicates and interacts is undergoing profound changes. Whereas in the old days, in scientific meetings and seminars, peers gravitated towards discipline clusters run as parallel sessions, these are now being increasingly supplemented by inter- and trans-disciplinary get-togethers mainly at the initiative of industry. But the sustainability of such emerging relationships as well as their meaningfulness and productivity can only be ensured by well-defined task-specific goals and fund support which encourages such behaviour patterns.

Shifts in the nature of scientific enquiry

The trend towards interdisciplinarity was triggered in the early 1960s when eminent physicists, chemists and mathematicians became interested by the exciting developments in biology. It would be fair to state that some of the major discoveries in modern biology were made by scientists brought up in unrelated disciplines. An example is illustrated by the history of nuclear magnetic resonance which, in the early days, diffused from physics, through chemistry to biology and to its current use in medical diagnosis. Probably the spread of ultra high resolution atomic force microscopy will similarly find application in as yet unanticipated fields. The shift may be seen not only in the gradual ascendancy of biology over physics but more generally in the shift of an ideal to which all sciences ought to aim. There is thus emerging a pluralism of approaches which combine data, methods and techniques from diverse sources to meet the requirements of specific contexts.

While the production of knowledge with practical ends in mind has always occupied an important place alongside gaining a better understanding of the physical and social world, continuous innovation to generate wealth through applying scientific and technological knowledge has reached a new level. Thus biosciences, material science and computer and information science, for instance, are now being driven by primary objectives of applications in mind. The current search to create the architecture of the fifth generation computers is driving much of the research into very large-scale integration of electronic switches, and to a small amount of the physics of semiconductors, or the mathematics of fuzzy logic. While many of the problems in these areas, by their very nature, generate an intrinsic intellectual interest for those who work on them, this interest is also continuously nourished by the research demands and practical interest of other users such as in genetics, electronics, mathematics and physics. Rather than pushing science into intellectually sterile backwaters, as some had feared, the expansion into ever new applications has begun to provide attractive and unusual challenges.[25]

One important fall-out of trans-disciplinary development is that it has for example become possible to reverse the conventional procedures for making new molecules or materials. Thus advances in combinatorial technologies now enable theoretical exploration of virtually unlimited permutations and combinations of new structures and reaction mechanisms, which would have been impossible to contemplate, leave aside undertake, using the traditional experimental methodologies. Such approaches become invaluable not only in terms of costs but more importantly, in terms of time and reduced adverse environmental impact, while opening up an entirely new range of socially relevant and wealth-generating possibilities.[28, 29, 30]

Information technology as an enabler

It is interesting that the technology which has achieved the maximum advance in this century has been the principal catalyst in the creation of knowledge networks around the world. The explosive growth of IT-related industries is well documented and makes news every day. Industries such as computers, electronic components, software development and telecommunications have already achieved dramatic reduction in costs and a counter-inflationary trend in prices, coupled with a galloping rise in technical performance. The inability of universities to anticipate the rate of change in IT has created a persistent shortage of skilled manpower in most of the developed economies. Consequently, this has progressively led to the mushrooming of extra academic institutions to generate skilled manpower outside the confines of academia. This probably has been a prime driving force for major IT companies in the West to create such manpower-developing institutions wherever in the world resources and conditions seemed to be appropriate. Thus the growth of the semiconductor industry in Malaysia and the software industry in India are two prominent examples of this type of global knowledge network.

The ability of MNC knowledge managers to generate more and more value from market opportunities is also well illustrated by the mushrooming growth of IT and industries related to it. As a matter of fact, without the explosive advances in IT and the dramatic drop in prices, the emergence of the powerful engine of collaborative partnership networks of scientific research resource would not have been possible. The ability to exchange, share, monitor and co-ordinate a myriad of geographically dispersed scientific activities, in real time, with resources dedicated in many instances to a single megascientific project, for instance the human genome project, has become a reality, entirely due to advances in IT and modern telephony.

The second but equally important role that IT is playing in the advancement of knowledge through scientific research is by providing a means to collate and distil meaningful and usable information from an unending flood of scientific and engineering data in publications and journals. The novelty lies in the speed of knowledge extraction, the quantity of raw data handled and the sharpness of the end product, which are so radically different compared to any other methods known to humankind (see below). These are the same processes which have led to the emergence of new scientific disciplines known collectively as 'combinatorial sciences'. Combinatorial disciplines now enable scientists to undertake theoretical exploration of virtually unlimited permutations and combinations of new molecular configurations and reaction mechanisms, before undertaking even a single table-top experiment. The sheer savings of time and experimental costs are so enormous that combinatorial techniques enable synthesis and tests with only a handful of target molecules of interest: a simplified process which could not have been contemplated even a few years ago. It is again the advances in IT, when adapted to the increasingly sophisticated field of measurement sciences, which now enable scientists to extract knowledge at the sub-atomic and *nano* resolution levels – measurement levels which could not have been imagined by the use of older techniques.

The visible as well as not so visible impact of advances in electronics and IT which has dramatically transformed the way we live and work is now all pervasive. It is the principal catalyst which is responsible for the spread and massification of education. It is therefore not surprising that such spread and massification, in turn, has given a new meaning to the concept of the management of knowledge for wealth creation. It is therefore not surprising that under these circumstances, among the MNCs, the IT and electronics majors have derived the greatest advantage to exploit their global reach via the information superhighway and thus gain unusual competitive advantages. There are naturally many valuable lessons arising from these pioneering initiatives of the IT industry for other firms and businesses on how to leverage new geographical opportunities, by linking and managing the information superhighway.

The other great benefit from IT to knowledge management is the emergence of strong inter- and trans-disciplinary methods of working.

At the individual level, the definition of what makes a good scientist was much more pluralistic. The freedom of individuals to make innovative choices, and design their own intellectual itineraries has increased dramatically. And scientific careers have once again, not unlike the early philosophers, constantly widening horizons of interest with the opportunity also to undergo frequent transformations. In this connection, one may recall an earlier reference to the fact that some of the major breakthroughs in the emerging disciplines of biochemistry were pioneered by physicists and mathematicians whose curiosity was triggered by both the logic as well as the complexities of nature. Similarly, many advances in modern surgery and medicine would not have been possible without the advances in engineering, electronics and design. What is happening in terms of interdisciplinarity today represents a change which is logarithmic in magnitude by comparison, with IT becoming the fundamental facilitator.

In this emerging paradigm, most scientific disciplines are showing increasing fuzziness at their boundaries. For example, biotechnology brings together biochemists, geneticists, chemical engineers, IT specialists, mathematicians, and so on. The human genome project requires the expertise of biology, chemistry and information processing. Molecular biology has not evolved according to any conventional disciplinary pattern because it has transformed the way questions are framed and research is undertaken in immunology, genetics or cell biology.

Other new fields such as risk or technology assessment also require experts from diverse fields to evolve objective outputs in the absence of which major agenda at national and international levels tend to be hijacked by amateurs. Thus the emergence of hybrid and to some extent transitional forms of new discipline need to be nurtured with great care during the evolutionary phase in order to maximise the knowledge and benefits these may yield. The power of the Internet, both to inform as well as to misinform, is now widely known.

In this environment, the gap between discipline-driven processes of imparting formal education is being further reinforced because it has become essential to provide the potential scientist with a strong underpinning in the basic sciences and mathematics. This is further widening the gap between the discipline of higher education and the interdisciplinary requirement for undertaking complex leading edge post-doctoral research. While this does not necessarily mean that there is any reduction in the requirement for synthetic organic chemists or microbiologists and so on, it does mean that excellence in mono-discipline has to be supplemented by acquiring certain multi-disciplinary skills in order to advance a meaningful scientific career either in academia or in industry. Unfortunately, there are no means as yet which would enable a gifted scientist to acquire multidisciplinary training formally.[25]

The type of individual who is likely to be successful in a career of scientific research has become remarkably different and several times more demanding than before. The vast number of PhDs and post-doctorals who have advanced through academia or industry via the research career, based on a basic training in a scientific discipline, are increasingly being relegated to the role of technicians, whereas those few who have the ability to seek the training and grasp the opportunity provided by an interdisciplinary horizon of knowledge creation, emerge as leaders of research in universities and industry. These changes are not only influencing and providing directions as to how future leaders of research may be trained but the complexity of a knowledge-driven society also creates a sense of apprehension among both politicians and business leaders. That advances in IT are determining the priorities of nation states, firms, and people in addition to influencing advances in science, underscores the future shape of knowledge generation and its use. The overarching role of IT pervades every element of this process and will continue to do so in the foreseeable future.

The Japanese way

We have discussed earlier that the emergence of the three-way collaborative configuration between universities, industry and government, in the developed Western world was for all intents and purposes absent in Japan. Like the West, Japan continued to invest massively in education, but ring-fenced the university system from its industrial development plans. In contrast the collaboration between the Japanese Government and its institutions on the one hand, and key sectors of Japanese industry on the other, were much more formal and stronger than anything witnessed in the West. In order to seek alternatives to the missing link with Japanese universities, many large Japanese corporations sought to invest and establish collaborations with leading universities in the West.

Such a stark difference in the generation and exploitation of knowledge in Japan is the subject of a recent book based on the research by Nonaka and Takeuchi.[24] While they have not explored the reasons for the isolation of Japanese universities, the hothouses of basic research, from Japanese industry, Nonaka and Takeuchi also do not claim that Japanese industries invest in fundamental research at the firm level in order to overcome this weakness. According to them,

> Japanese companies have become successful because of their skills and expertise at *organisational knowledge creation* – a capability of a company as a whole to create new knowledge, disseminate it throughout the organisation and embody it in products, services and systems. (p. viii)

One is left with an impression that probably Japan has mastered the art of synthesis and exploitation of existing knowledge sources better than any other country. In explaining the 'Japanese way', Nonaka and Takeuchi make an important distinction between *explicit knowledge*, which can be articulated in formal language, including grammatical statements, mathematical expressions, specifications, manuals and so forth and which, according to Nonaka and Takeuchi, is the dominant mode of codifying knowledge in the Western philosophical tradition, and the more important kind of knowledge, *tacit knowledge,* which is hard to articulate with formal language. They describe it as personal knowledge embedded in individual experience and involving intangible factors such as personal belief, perspective and the value system. Nowhere do the authors refer to the most vital source of new knowledge which originates in basic research or the power of emerging interdisciplinarity with which to exploit knowledge in the creation of wealth.

Undoubtedly, the Japanese organisational culture and behaviour have been generally acknowledged as being superior to those prevalent in the West, and are a key to the distinctive ways that Japanese companies innovate. But how do Japanese companies sustain continuous innovation? Japanese companies have traditionally turned to their suppliers, customers, distributors, government agencies and even competitors for new insights or clues they might provide, claim Nonaka and Takeuchi. In order to support their observations, they quote extensively but exclusively from Western authors such as Drucker,[31] Toffler,[32] Quinn[33] and Reich[34] to underline a central theme that knowledge is the only meaningful resource to generate wealth and drive competitiveness. In contrast, their contention is that the

Japanese way of creating knowledge within the corporations is different and is what distinguishes Japanese companies.

Since explicit knowledge is universal, the authors emphasise that *tacit* knowledge and its exploitation is what makes Japanese companies more successful. In a 1998 news article, Peter Drucker[35] likened tacit knowledge to attempts to write a manual which might self-teach a novice how to ride a bicycle from scratch. The process is obviously difficult to manualise for someone to learn from. There are several such human skills and competencies which can be thus classified under a general heading of *ability*. Levitt[36] points out:

> The most precious knowledge can neither be taught nor passed on. (p. 17)

And this is what Nonaka and Takeuchi claim that the Japanese undertake to manage organisationally, an ability which the West leaves to individuals to make use of as best they can.

The explanation of how Japanese companies create new knowledge boils down to the transformation of *tacit knowledge* to *explicit knowledge by human team endeavour*. And in the Japanese system, new knowledge is claimed to be born out of chaos rather than orderly exploration and enquiry.

Incidentally, most of the research reported in this book on Japanese knowledge management was conducted in the 1980s. At the time the Japanese economy was strong and Japanese companies loomed like competitive juggernauts on the world stage. Japan stood as the paragon of new economic management and the way it managed knowledge held some unique lessons for the rest of the world. Today, the Japanese economy is in serious trouble and Japanese companies appear considerably less invincible. Whether this new vulnerability also has anything to do with the recent trend among the Japanese universities seeking to forge closer collaboration with Japanese industries, with the active encouragement and support of the Japanese government, remains unclear.

Nonaka and Takeuchi arrive at a somewhat ambiguous but nevertheless tantalising conclusion that organised human interaction to transform tacit knowledge into explicit knowledge holds the key to competitive success in innovation. This is in stark contrast to the generally held view that organised human endeavour to generate knowledge is catalysed by scientific research, and that interdisciplinary exploitation of such knowledge leads to sustained creation of wealth.

Knowledge and market forces

The driving force behind the accelerated supply and demand for marketable knowledge lies in the intensification of international competition in business and industry. One key driving force is the ceaseless reconfiguration of resources, knowledge and skills. According to Gibbons *et al.*,[25] knowledge-intensive companies remain highly profitable because they possess skills not found elsewhere, including brokering skills which are necessary to link problem solvers and problem identifiers. The increased market attractiveness of science is due to the fact that those who possess specific scientific skills are willing to be brought together, even in temporary interdisciplinary teams, to work on difficult and challenging problems. Alfred North Whitehead observed many years ago that the brilliance of the nineteenth century was not the discovery of any particular invention but the discovery of the method of invention. In the late twentieth century, both supply and demand for such discoveries and inventions have expanded and accelerated along with the creation of new conditions and places for making them.

With the traditional economic activities rapidly spreading beyond the West and Japan into emerging markets, manufacturing and trading are now being supplemented by knowledge management to enable the developed economies to sustain their leadership and pre-eminence in technological innovations.[37] Thus knowledge provides the link to occupy the space created by a shift from trading skills to technological skills. In other words, one may compare the seafaring skills of the trading communities of the past centuries with the emerging skills of knowledge surfing along modern information superhighways, with a single purpose to achieve superior economic advantage – a historic preoccupation of humankind.

But even among firms in the developed economies, differences exist in their ability to commercialise knowledge, while competitive advantage lies with those that are successful in doing so. In a way, knowledge management is emerging as the new index to measure longevity of firms as well as the basis for many mergers and acquisitions, for example in the pharmaceutical industry and in the financial services. The competency of successful firms, under these conditions is marked by a number of attributes. Thus many of them demonstrate the ability to generate knowledge using resources which are not all stored in-house but distributed throughout a vast and expanding global network. They create new links with universities, government laboratories and even other firms. All these, to remain manageable, goal-orientated and measurable, require the firm to match them with well-defined market forces and opportunities. Under such circumstances, commercialisation is more complex compared to the historic linear model, where science leads to technology and technology fulfils market needs.

Technology is no longer a commodity available 'off-the-shelf', nor can it be accessed through technology transfer or intellectual property agreements alone. While all of these skills exist in different parts of the world, invariably they turn out to be sub-optimal and non-competitive except under monopoly conditions. The generation and application of knowledge to meet specific market opportunity requires management competencies of a totally different order of magnitude. Industry's preoccupation with economies of scale in manufacturing and distribution is now shifting to include production of scientific and technological knowledge. Economies of scope are being built into the firm-level *supply circle* where market demand is met by continuous innovations driven by knowledge, derived from dynamic science and technology formulations. Inexorably, the constantly changing nature of competition is shifting the focus of added value in the innovation process towards a firm's competence in configuring knowledge resources.

Some key drivers

One key driver of the various changes described in the previous sections, is the reduction of the half-life of innovations. While innovation half-life on an average was 15–20 years in the early 1960s, the half-life of innovations has progressively dropped to around five years in the 1990s and is expected to keep dropping further in the future. Successful firms of the future will be judged by their innovation intensity more than ever before. Furthermore, most of the innovation will be based on superior understanding of markets but derived primarily from the commercial exploitation of knowledge derived from science and technology. Thus, in knowledge production, industrialisation of scientific research may be described in terms of adoption of economies of scale and new industrial management practices.

Such new management practices are needed both within the firm and in dealing with potential knowledge partners. For example, while there are many university and government laboratories with large and sophisticated technological systems which demand huge investments and modern management, so far, with some notable exceptions, these new management practices are missing. Therefore, the availability of research results for social and economic benefits has been severely restricted. Industrial collaboration and partnership with such institutions are now rapidly rising. For such relationships to be sustainable and productive means that, invariably, industry has to superimpose management discipline without unduly curbing the traditional strengths of such universities and institutions. More often than not, both industry and government are surprised to discover, in such partnerships, vast amounts of information and knowledge already available in universities, much of which becomes instantly applicable and which encourages investments in longer-term scientific programmes.

Competitive activity is another important driver in the pursuit of knowledge. Its effect in reducing the half-life of innovation has already been mentioned. While forecasting emerging events from market forces alone continues to be surrounded by high background noise, monitoring key competitive activities and advances in technologies relevant to a particular firm can help develop more accurate forecasts. Just as nature poses questions for science, markets continuously pose questions to the firm. Innovations provide the answer. The firm's response thus acquires an exploratory character driven entirely by its competence and the quality of its knowledge base.

The commerce of knowledge production

> The accumulation of capital, insofar as it involves the creation of technological knowledge, takes place inside the firms, but the rate of that accumulation is related to the extent to which the firm has access to knowledge generated by others.[31] (p. 8)

Thus it becomes clear that if it is to survive, a firm must specialise. This provides an extended dimension to the concept of core competency propounded by Hamel and Prahalad.[38] Companies which sharply define what constitutes their core competency and then reinforce this by highly directed access to their knowledge needs tend to remain highly profitable because they develop and nurture skills which are not found everywhere. According to Reich,[34] the presence of non-imitable knowledge-dependent firms can be found throughout the manufacturing industry, whether firms are large or small, whether they are young or old or whether their technologies are mature or at the leading edge. Traditional service industries are also re-engineering themselves by utilising specialised knowledge. The telecommunication revolution was triggered by an explosion of new knowledge and subsequently created integrated networks for transportation services such as road, rail, air freight and shipping, providing an entirely new definition to economies of scale and scope. The revolution in international financial services is changing the concept of money and its use in unanticipated ways.

It is obvious that skills required to weave knowledge into traditional systems and methods to create a new set of competencies are indeed entirely different from traditional skills and traditional ways of problem solving. Since these skills do not arise spontaneously and are going to be in increasing demand, they pose a challenge to existing systems of higher education. Nonaka and Takeuchi[24] have described this as building an organisational culture to exploit *tacit knowledge* and which, according to them, underlines the innovation strengths of Japanese companies and is a reason for their superior performance, as described in the previous section. In the West, competency in innovation is being redefined in terms of ability to solve problems by selecting relevant data and skills and organising them appropriately. When information is plentiful, perhaps too plentiful, competence does not derive from being able to generate yet more, but from the ability to distil what is meaningful in novel ways. This notion of competence may be somewhat similar to what the Japanese term as *tacit knowledge*. If this interpretation can be substantiated, it may help develop a new cadre of specialists who emerge as problem identifiers and solution managers or co-ordinators. This has already started to have a large effect on organisational structures, cultures and behaviours. Like innovation, the half-life of organisational structure is also reducing rapidly. By the 1980s, the concept of profit centres and SBUs were well entrenched into organisational structures, as a preamble to sharpen the definition of core competency. With the explosive growth of IT, and when the corporate centre's Big Blue computers were replaced by distributed desktop units all across firms, information overflow became a real problem. The emergence of a chief information officer was a means to provide some order and discipline grafted on to existing organisation structure. Simultaneously, there was already underway a silent, knowledge revolution. Many business heads and industry research directors felt overwhelmed by the pace of change of events. Again, someone came up with the idea first of a chief technology officer and, more recently, that of a chief knowledge officer. All these were grafted alongside old organisation structures with the expectations that such individuals may be able to weave knowledge and its technical accoutrements into the fabric of the firm without shaking the old order too violently. Of course, as is becoming evident, while all these new measures are partially worthwhile, competitive advantage can only be derived by empowering individual managers and decision makers themselves to deal with all aspects of knowledge, driven by business needs rather than remaining dependent on specialists. In other words, knowledge and its exploitation has become a prerequisite qualification for all professional managers rather than a domain to be managed by specialists.

While at the firm level, it is now being gradually acknowledged that managers need skills and competencies to deal with both *explicit* and *tacit* knowledge to drive the companies' core competencies, most companies have come to realise that such specialised training for individuals is not a part of higher education in most countries, nor is it in the core curriculum in most leading business schools. Until such time that knowledge as a learning component is built into academic curricula, it will have to be imparted by individual firms through management training and development of new as well as experienced senior managers. Second, since the knowledge pool of a firm is made up of its in-house resources as well as that accessed through partnerships with universities and research institutions, managers have the additional task to share the firm level learning with its external partners as a value-creating imperative.

Evolving some measures

Well-thought-out and well-planned management intervention to raise the quality and productivity of the science and technology networks, formed with external partners, has started changing the way in which industrial R&D as well as academic research is assessed. The claim of academic scientific excellence as measured by publications, citation indices, peer ratings, and so on was considered as the primary and overriding criterion for judging the quality of knowledge produced, and hence that of the knowledge producer. This was the basis for the insistence of academic freedom, protected from any other form of scrutiny or assessment. In industry, by contrast, traditionally the key measures were entirely different, such as patents, first to market and business (funding source) assessment of worth and value. Peer rating and publications were important but of secondary value in judging the quality of knowledge produced in industry. Other research institutions and government R&D institutes tended to adopt a hybrid of measures drawing a bit from both. In the United States some pioneering attempts were made, mainly by funding agencies, to introduce certain quantitative measures to judge the quality of knowledge produced as well as to assess funding priorities. But the real change was triggered by the advent of venture capitalism which utilised the conversion of knowledge into wealth creation as a prime measure of value.

Progressively, it became obvious that new and common measures had to be devised so that the partnership between industry, university and government laboratories could be assessed on a common scale without sacrificing, too much, some of the inherent strengths of each. Industry is naturally having to lead in formulating and laying down guidelines for measurement because its survival depends on workable and harmonious external partners. A common scale is the only way which will enable different constituents in a knowledge partnership to speak the same language of monitoring and evaluation.

As the number of participants in any knowledge production project increases, so does the number of centres in the network set up for the purpose. Such large initiatives are extremely sensitive to changes that inevitably occur in different social, economic and technical environments. This potentially means high risk, high volatility and increased uncertainty. The time when planning meant operations research-based output of a series of milestones with in-built options has passed. Increasingly, the conceptualisation, selection and realisation of future options are beset by uncertainties or can only be ascertained experimentally in the course of doing the actual research. This is, of course, highly unsatisfactory as recently witnessed in handling the scientific evaluation of BSE in the UK, the rising incidents of food poisoning generally or the appearance of oestrogen-type compounds in the environment.

At the firm level, the creation of task-based knowledge networks is providing new opportunities for participants confidently to undertake the complex exercise of planning, design, risk assessment and so on, on a project-by-project basis. This way of innovation management clearly delineates accountability, time, cost and risk aspects across a firm as well as between project network partners. Transparency, clear accountability and IT-based decision support systems are raising the chances of success of all knowledge-driven projects, defining priorities and making risks much more manageable with the help of early warning methodologies (see Chapter 5). In a different context, is the role played by public controversies related to products and services created by emerging knowledge and expertise. It is worth exploring some of these public policy implications, since they have a direct bearing on the future of business and economic performance. To cite a few examples, one may include industrial development and global warming, human genetic information and insurance premium procedures of genetically modified agricultural products and many, many others. Thus the very transparency of the knowledge networks provides a good basis for risk assessment in the context of social concern and provides a new and powerful tool for firms to assess, fairly early on, the impact of their investment decisions around the world. It is now becoming increasingly common to share company plans and programmes for new products and processes with public interest groups in different markets, quite in contrast to the tradition of corporate secrecy. Academic institutions wishing to preserve their independence from any questioning whatsoever, public or otherwise, are also facing similar demands. The current debate on the desirability, or otherwise, of genetically modified seeds provides an interesting backdrop to the ongoing argument between a company like Monsanto and organised groups opposed to genetic engineering.

Assessing some contemporary issues

In view of the various exciting developments described above, it is worth exploring certain aspects of how knowledge management works in actual practice, in the form of an illustrative narrative.

It is necessary to appreciate that while knowledge management may be complex as a theoretical concept, there is nothing profound about its application in practice. The purpose of describing some of its more practical aspects is to reassure those who are joining the game late, that even they can catch up, because certain modern technology competencies, if acquired, can enable a firm to leapfrog across large time spans.

There is sometimes a tendency to relate the term *knowledge management* to the dawn of the modern *information age*. Nothing could be farther from reality. It is sobering to contemplate that knowledge is as old as humankind and human evolution has been driven by the use and application of knowledge. Knowledge is the motivating force for comprehension and the catalyst for all social and economic development. What modern technology has provided is the fuel to accelerate the pace of change and make knowledge freely available around the world.

Knowledge emanates from *all* human activity. In business, the important sources include the marketplace, in R&D and what may be stored in recorded or unrecorded corporate archives. The ability to weave all these sources into a fabric of opportunities, and thus create competitive advantages at the firm level, is what successful knowledge management is all about.

Companies which plan and successfully manage knowledge invariably derive significant competitive advantages and marketplace leadership. This has been demonstrated in virtually every sphere of economic activity ranging from agriculture to manufacturing to the service industries. Furthermore, the whole area of strategic defence management is entirely knowledge driven and was one of the key factors in the winding down of the cold war which had gripped the world for over 40 years. Achievements in world agriculture production and productivity are other powerful examples of the use of modern knowledge management. The next phase in the agricultural revolution will be spurred by knowledge generated from advances in biotechnology. As a matter of fact, biotechnology is likely to provide solutions which may reduce or eliminate dependence on agrochemicals and fertilisers and thus dramatically lower the ecological load generated by global agricultural activities. Similarly, the debate on global warming will eventually have to seek solutions from the industrial knowledge base rather than from political bargaining and manipulation. In the manufacturing sphere, to cite a more contemporary example, the world dominance of the Japanese automotive industry was primarily knowledge driven, combining what the consumer wanted with superior technology in design and engineering, while the explosion in information technology spewed out of the knowledge mines of Silicon Valley. In the sphere of services, knowledge has been the key to the modernisation of international banking and transactions in stocks and shares, while the expanding horizons of satellite linkages have permanently altered the business of telephony. The access to or lack of knowledge makes all the difference between a successful tourism and travel business from their underperforming counterparts. Finally, the most obvious and comprehensive example of man's knowledge-driven achievements is in the sphere of new drug discovery and modern health care.

The issue that remains somewhat speculative is what happens to societies which are not equipped either to comprehend or manage to ramp-up the increasing demands of social engineering. Many social activists and some intellectuals may advise the disadvantaged to 'go back to nature'. But even to go back to nature and seek sustainable livelihood requires a higher level of competence in manoeuvring and manipulating knowledge than one generally assumes.

The price of deliberate or unconscious incompetence can be very high, as recently demonstrated in some of the East European and Tiger Asian economies. While there is no generic pattern which has emerged from the severe financial set-backs in South Korea, Malaysia, Thailand, Indonesia and so on, as yet, it is obvious that the knowledge-based regulatory checks and balances in most of these countries were inadequate to warn against the financial overheating which most of these economies encountered. While demand-driven economic growth is more manageable, when this becomes competition driven, the quality of competencies needed is of a different order of magnitude. The South Korean 'Chaebols' are very interesting examples of growth and diversification, which were not entirely knowledge driven. Although, in recent times, there has been growing criticism of the concept of core competence as being restrictive of leadership, vision and growth aggression, there is now mounting evidence that the validity of the concept of core competence is fundamentally the product of corporate knowledge and its management. The metamorphosis of the *Fortune 500* over the years is probably the best example of how large global conglomerates of unrelated businesses have gradually given way to large global companies, whose core competence is well defined by their corporate knowledge competency.

As already mentioned, the OECD countries now have adopted an active policy that large investment must be allocated to the development of knowledge workers even during periods of low economic growth. Even this does not guarantee lifetime employment with its consequent fall-out on social security costs and national level competitiveness. In global trade, the WTO as a successor to the Uruguay pact has as its sole aim to protect and provide competitive advantage to those who can sustainably generate and use knowledge, particularly in the transaction of multinational commerce. Thus, while the Uruguay pact provided a certain balance by taking into account the differences in competencies of nations, the WTO aims to narrow or eliminate any preferential concessions.

In this scenario, the growing economies of Asia and Latin America will continue to sustain their advances only if they dedicate resources to develop and supply increasing numbers of knowledge workers which their growth plans will demand. India and China are in very similar situations. While China has clearly laid down plans to raise its national competencies by maximum investment in education and institution building, India, which is probably better endowed in terms of established institutions and human resources, has yet to take advantage of her rich natural advantages.

It is in the light of some of these contemporary developmental issues that one needs to view the critical importance of knowledge and its management to achieve competitive leadership and in wealth creation.

Knowledge at the firm level

How knowledge management works at the firm level is fairly simple in terms of a concept. The complexity arises in the *process* of transforming knowledge into goods and services. This section briefly deals with certain aspects of the process and its dynamics. The two key sources of knowledge in firms are customer/market information and the R&D departments. These two also happen to be very strongly interconnected. Thus, to convert customers' demand into goods and services which fulfils a particular demand, with the use of knowledge, represents a firm-level opportunity. Any competitive advantage in delivering such goods and services can only be instilled by weaving the results from scientific research and technology development into products. The ability to protect the knowledge thus generated in the form of intellectual property of the firm, ensures a measure of exclusive and profitable longevity.

All businesses work on the assumption that their *raison d'être* depends upon their profound understanding of the reasons behind the demand for their goods and services. The science of marketing and market research is indeed complex because it has to deal with human behaviour at the individual, community and national levels. The majority of business failures or set-backs can be traced to incomplete or inadequate understanding of marketplace dynamics. Some of the recent and better known examples are those of Philips, IBM, AT&T, among others. But even those who understand the profundity of consumer demands and market trends have to be constantly on their toes because of the rapid shifts which take place almost continuously, and as a result of which today's success can become tomorrow's liability. Furthermore, a strong understanding of the opportunities will not automatically translate into sales, without the help of leading-edge R&D, and which is in tune with an agile and responsive supply chain.

In this seamless link, connecting market opportunities to R&D and the supply chain, knowledge is the key component which runs as a continuum. Furthermore, while there is a rich seam of published work on the role of market research, consumer understanding and the supply chain, the impact of R&D, although acknowledged as an act of faith, is probably least well understood as a process. There are notable exceptions of course in the chemical, pharmaceutical and electronics industries, but even in these there are some glaring disjunctions between the marketplace and the R&D laboratory.

There are several reasons for this state of affairs. One principal reason is the traditional gaps between academic, institutional and industrial R&D. Second, the conceptual distinction between high technology, low technology, and no technology in classifying different economic activities meant that somehow the high technology firms were considered to be more R&D dependent compared to the other two categories. This artificial distinction was reinforced by the capital intensity of the chemical, pharmaceutical and electronic firms, whose large R&D budgets and some of their visible successes perpetrated this myth. Such beliefs were also underscored by management practices in certain service industries. For example, until not very long ago disciplines such as hospital and hotel management were considered as the exclusive domains of doctors and chefs.

A combination of factors has helped destroy such historical myths. First, information technology established beyond any doubt that the speed and value of information had made *all* firms technology dependent, and the second was that the speed of developments in science was advancing at such a pace that it was no longer possible for any single firm to undertake, in-house, all or even the bulk of R&D to meet its business objectives. A third, and not insignificant, factor was that the cost and complexity of academic research have risen to levels which can no longer, with few exceptions, be supported by the taxpayer's money alone. Some of the pioneering and profound trans-formations in attitudes and practices began in the USA, giving birth to, among other things, technology entrepreneurship and venture capitalism in and around American campuses. These pioneering prac-tices have now begun to spread roots in the EU. Surprisingly, in the most innovative of nations, Japan, the separation between academia and industry was very strictly maintained until very recently, while venture capitalism and academia/industrial collaboration remains minimal even today.

Since information technology is the pump that primed the new industrial revolution and since this, in turn, has driven industrial R&D from the back rooms to the boardrooms, understanding the R&D process has become invaluable to the progress of any world-class busi-ness. This is discussed in detail in Chapter 5.

The knowledge pyramid

This section deals with some mechanics of managing the *sources* and *uses* of knowledge. Before describing some practical aspects, it is useful to select a working definition of knowledge appropriate in the context of this chapter

The *Oxford English Dictionary* gives four definitions of the verb 'to know'. These are:

■ to have in only mind or memory as a result of learning or information

■ to feel certain

■ to recognise with certainty

■ to understand and be able to use.

For the purposes of this narrative, 'to understand and be able to use' most closely relates to the subject at hand. Even this definition is in a way incomplete because it leaves out probably the most vital activity, 'to create or to generate or to synthesise'. And this is where the dynamics have most profoundly changed. The change in every sphere of scientific activity continues to progress at an exponential rate. Under these circumstances, the ability of the socioeconomic sciences as well as some consequential public policy issues to keep pace with the generation of new scientific knowledge has been seriously strained. Whether in human genetics or in public health or in matters concerning the environment, the speed of new discoveries and the explosion of new events have left the politician, the policy makers and the lay public befuddled, bewildered and truculent. Scientists are now looked upon with a degree of suspicion rather than the traditional awe. The faith in governments has eroded similarly, and now there is a universal 'desire to get a handle on' and 'to understand and be able to use' issues in the minds of the public. The ongoing controversies range from mad cow disease, cloning of animals and human embryos, use of genetically modified crops in food products to global warming – just to cite a few examples once again. Probably the most immediate preoccupation with the *millennium bomb* is a telling example of incomplete knowledge built into the electronic software and hardware developed only a few decades ago and which, if not solved in time, has the potential to spread universal chaos. Even the cost of a partial solution in a country like the UK is estimated to be of the order of £50 billion. In spite of all the problems, it remains a fact that our world can continue on its evolutionary journey only by generation, comprehension and sensible use of new knowledge spewing out of explosive discoveries in science and technology.

The information explosion in the wake of the advances in *information technology* and *telephony* is forcing people around the world to explore ways and means to separate what we need to 'understand and be able to use' from the vast amount of raw data and information mountains under which it lies buried. One may distinguish data and information as a 'feedstock' from which to extract desired 'products' – metaphorically somewhat akin to cracking and distilling hydrocarbon to obtain desired fractions. While this was a useful analogy to communicate with IT specialists, what eventually emerged as a layman's working model is in the shape of a knowledge pyramid as shown in Figure 3.1.

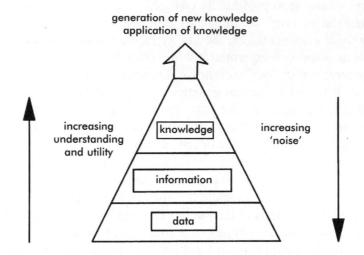

Figure 3.1   The knowledge pyramid

Figuratively, the base of the pyramid is made up of raw data or 'feedstock'. Separating usable information from such a 'feedstock' is the first step in a clarification process. The distinguishing feature of *usable information* is that it can lead to the crystallisation and application of relevant knowledge. This rather simple description provides a powerful management tool in the day-to-day use of knowledge at the firm level. Similar applications at a societal or a national level still remain relatively under-explored.

One may now begin to understand why the explosive growth in IT has tended to blur the distinction between *data*, *information* and *knowledge*. For instance, the progressive unravelling and understanding of the human genome is spewing out enormous amounts of *data*. Extracting *information* from these data has yet to progress beyond a handful of a few well-publicised applications. But the *knowledge* which will eventually dominate all future medical and pharmaceutical research, and completely revolutionise medical science, remains a distant dream. Similar is the case of speculation with regard to global warming and the chaotic climatic phenomenon named El Niño. Mountains of *data* are being gathered round the clock by climatologists around the world, the *information* from these data is equally impressive, but the *knowledge* required to deal with the consequences of the vagaries of the El Niño phenomenon remains utterly obscure. There have been bold attempts to explain some of it by the application of the science of chaos. But whether it is application of fractal mathematics or the campaigns by Greenpeace, neither is based on the *knowledge* which will eventually permit both the comprehension and approach to objective solutions of such global problems.

The acquisition and application of new knowledge does not get better just by using new or more powerful computer technology or accumulating even more data. This is unfortunately, however, what specialists tend to concentrate upon. While it must be admitted that this approach provided the basics for the first-generation software developments and 'artificial intelligence' applications, their use has been limited by being somewhat mechanistic and restrictive. In contrast, the 'distillation' of raw data requires the 'user' to pose the right questions (temperature and pressure, for example, in the chemical engineer's jargon) to the IT specialists so that a user-specified boundary condition can be developed and put to use.

Knowledge in industry

I would now like briefly to discuss some specific aspects of the application of knowledge in the industrial sphere. In doing this, I propose to restrict myself to R&D in industry which is the subject of this book. The applications to other business areas such as finance, marketing and manufacturing are not only equally important but are also all interconnected in the form of a holistic management process. But each of these also happens to be discrete disciplines, which need to be dealt with as individual topics, aspects which I do not propose to deal with in this book. Similarly, issues which relate to other day-to-day activities in society and which are deeply influenced by knowledge, still remain to be fully explored and recorded.

The practice of R&D in industry is fairly old and well established in the developed countries. It is undertaken as a primary source of wealth and power. Historically, there has always been a distance and distinction between R&D in universities and R&D in industry. Stand-alone contract research organisations or national R&D institutions tended to be more closely aligned to industry. There has been a somewhat leisurely and uncharted pace of change in these traditional alignments. Universities were traditionally funded by the state and developed the trained scientific human resources dedicated primarily to generate knowledge and secondarily to create wealth. Dominant corporations were able to protect their intellectual property and become market leaders by using these human resources developed in universities. In recent years, two fundamental developments have changed this scenario. First, as mentioned elsewhere, the half-life of new discoveries and innovation dropped dramatically, being rapidly overtaken by newer discoveries and newer innovations. In other words, the rate of obsolescence of usable knowledge accelerated. Second, the state funding of universities was no longer sufficient to meet their needs, even in rich countries, and supplementary sources had to be found. Such a situation provided the ideal conditions to break the historic separation of academia from industry and hence the marketplace. (The oft-expressed fears that such trespass into ivory towers would harm creativity and blue-sky explorations have not been borne out by events.) Furthermore, because no single industry is any longer capable of undertaking on its own all the R&D it needs for its business, primarily because of the speed of progress in science and technology, industry is forced to seek new formations of partnership/ alliance with academia to sustain a critical knowledge mass, while still retaining a desired degree of exclusivity.

The funding problems of scientific education and academic research along with advances in IT and telephony, provide the positive impetus to seek a grand alliance between industry and academia, in order to generate faster and greater quantities of relevant knowledge in order to gain competitive advantage and thus to create wealth.

The process of exploiting science for wealth creation, has gained unprecedented momentum in the advanced countries and has permanently changed the way R&D is beginning to be managed in these nations. In simple terms, there has been a holistic shift in the *knowledge universe* from isolation and compartmentalisation towards integration and strategic partnerships.

The knowledge universe

Although traditionally there have always been direct and indirect links between the various constituents among knowledge generators and users, the information highway has rendered these links transparent, transactional and, therefore, sustainable. This probably can best be visualised as shown in Figure 3.2.

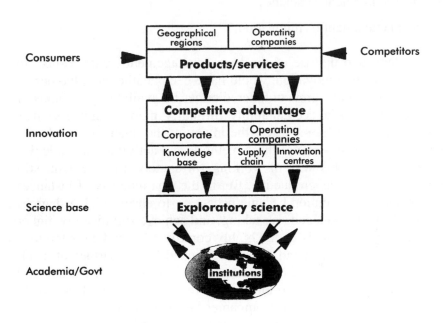

Figure 3.2   The knowledge universe

I hope the dynamic flow pattern around the 'Universe' is apparent from the map itself, aided by a combination of speed of technological change and information explosion, which are permanently influencing the way knowledge is generated, harnessed and utilised. Information from the marketplace streams in at one end while new knowledge from the world of science flows in at the other. Such a state of continuous flow creates a permanent state of turbulence and can either lead to chaos if left alone to manage itself, or give birth to some unique opportunities if managed purposefully, competently and comprehensively.

I will now briefly describe some of the tools which have evolved and have been developed for the purposeful and competent harnessing of knowledge using the knowledge universe as a model. The two key management activities which have a profound influence on the knowledge dynamics mentioned above are:

- the management of science
- the management of innovation.

Not so long ago the use of the term 'management', with respect to both science and innovation, would have been anathema to the purist. Historically, science grew unfettered either by availability of funds or commercial or social accountability. Similarly, innovation was seen as the domain of the free-spirited, the inventor, the loner in the 'skunkworks'. Of course, some of these methods and activities have a legitimate space and this way of working fortunately, to an extent, still prevails and remains productive. But in the vast majority of instances management intervention became necessary to ensure higher degrees of confidence in managed risk-taking, and achieve significantly higher rates of success. This is both a highly controversial and a contentious subject and I do not intend to be sidetracked by the virtues of academic freedom and isolation, compared to academic freedom and accountability. Suffice it to understand that events around the world are moving so rapidly for companies as well as nations, that for sustainable achievements, management intervention and leadership has become essential for both.

Managing science, technology and innovation

In the commercial context it is possible to visualise a *knowledge chain* which links science to the marketplace (Figure 3.3).

It is now worthwhile briefly to describe each of the components which jointly make up a firm's knowledge chain (see Chapter 5).

Science themes

Each firm or corporation has a unique set of requirements for continuous flow of knowledge with which to fuel business growth and sustain its competitive intensity. Individual corporations have therefore carefully to plot the area of fundamental science they need to match their long-term business vision. Typically each firm has to develop a profile of its future requirements from science, which nowadays more and more tend to be interdisciplinary. Such interdisciplinary but discrete clusters of scientific activities emerge as core themes at the firm level. Such themes by their very nature tend to be dynamic. What distinguishes them from an amorphous collection of traditional scientific disciplines is the requirement of in-depth understanding of advances taking place in various areas of new interdisciplinary sciences and the firm's ability to sustain a leading-edge competence over long periods. This can be done only by continuous scrutiny and corrections in order to be able to remain at the leading edge.

The knowledge chain – weaving science into innovation

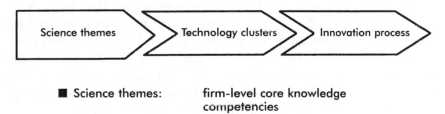

- Science themes: firm-level core knowledge competencies
- Technology clusters: vehicle to convert discoveries into usable entities
- Innovation projects: deliver business growth and leadership

Figure 3.3   The knowledge chain

Thus chosen science themes become firm- or business-specific choices of knowledge-generators through scientific explorations. For example, in the pharmaceutical industry science themes would include disciplines such as biotechnology, combinatorial chemistry, human physiology, safety science, and so on. In contrast, say, in the automobile industry key themes would include material science, engineering sciences, virtual reality designing, and so on. As mentioned earlier, because of explosive advances in every area of fundamental science, the only way a firm can build and sustain a *critical mass* in its sphere of interest or themes is through a formal network of partnerships with appropriate academic leaders and institutions. The process by which a firm defines its need of critical mass conditions is by measuring the rate of flow of fundamental knowledge from a set of preordained activities and with which to fuel its knowledge chain. This subject is treated in greater detail in Chapter 5.

Technology clusters

Technology clusters represent utilisable entities of fundamental knowledge flowing in from a critical mass of related scientific research. Such utilisable technologies, in turn, represent one of the core competencies of a firm and constitute its usable knowledge base. Such competencies underpin a firm's ability to fuel its innovation machine for product and process developments, driven by well-defined parameters of business opportunities and priorities. To sustain the 'calorific' quality and value of the innovation engine, both the critical mass of the science base as well as the quality of utilisable technology clusters have to be carefully and continuously orchestrated.

Innovation process

Successful innovations are the practical expression of end products achieved by transforming business-defined market opportunities into tradable goods and services with the help of outputs from appropriate science and their utilisable technology. It is, therefore, apparent that management of the innovation process at the firm level is the ultimate process of knowledge exploitation to gain competitive advantage and market leadership (see Chapter 5).

Through a looking glass

The use and application of knowledge as well as its quality will remain, in the foreseeable future, dependent upon the tools used to 'crack' and 'distil' information. In order for individuals or groups to do this with increasing confidence and consistency, the only method available is that of continuous learning, in order to retain their skills at the leading edge. The historic practice of receiving a formal education and then embarking on a life-long professional career, interspersed with occasional training events, has become more or less obsolete. The concept of a 'life-long' career itself has become outdated even in paternalistic cultures such as Japan. Formal education now at best equips an individual with the basic minimum skills to embark upon a career. The progress through working life is determined by an individual's ability continuously to renew his or her skills. Although this was, to a certain extent, true even in former times, it was at best described by an arbitrary value put on an attribute called 'experience'. Because of the rapid changes in the knowledge and technology universe, experience, at best, has been reduced to an entity of partial value. It has now to be supplemented by elements of continuous learning and renewal of skills. This makes very heavy demands on any individual – not everyone is able to cope with such demands – and has brought to an end the era of life-long employment. On the positive side, such workplace demands have generated a sense of greater self-esteem and confidence among the majority of individuals at all work levels in a firm. And the important consequence is the demise of the old style supervisory roles and delayering of organisational structures. Similarly, the traditional we–they roles of employees and managers are being gradually replaced by we – the winning team in many genuinely modern learning organisations. Many of these ideas and practices would have been branded as starry-eyed in the 1970s and 80s, while today they have become essential practices for the survival of any business.

Corporate cultural changes driven by knowledge are indeed profound. Once an organisation is successful in adopting a culture of renewal, its leadership is set free from the day-to-day operations in order to envision change, seek new opportunities and deal with challenges, ahead of its competition, and thus undertake genuine leadership roles. This enables such a corporation comprehensively to beat competition consistently, enlarge itself by mergers and acquisitions

(M&A) while continuously lowering costs and improving profits. *Economies of scale have begun to be displaced by economies of knowledge.*

In this heady environment we get excited watching two-year-olds playing with a computer mouse and keyboard. This may be good for the psyche of parents and for the sellers of computer games, but how can we be sure that these new instruments of learning are not the steam engines of tomorrow? As the well-known saying goes, the only constant is change. What does all this mean for countries which have yet to comprehend the impact of the new knowledge universe? Two recent studies are quite revealing in this regard. An American study explored why the 1952 Silicon Valley phenomenon could not be repeated as successfully elsewhere in the USA, let alone anywhere else in the world! The conclusion from a comparative analysis of several technology parks in the USA revealed that Silicon Valley provided an almost accidental combination of a leading university, an entrepreneurial critical mass and an enlightened local administration, just at the right time which happened to be appropriate to ignite a knowledge revolution. Trying to reproduce this at many other locations such as the Triangle Park in North Carolina, or in Bethesda, Maryland, and so on turned out to be not exactly as rewarding. To this day there is no clear answer why Silicon Valley worked; there are, of course, several opinions. The other study was comparison of factors which led to the emergence of Bangalore as a leading software centre, and comparing these with plans of some of the Tiger economies to create much grander centres in Malaysia and Singapore. This comparative work which was done at Stanford University concludes that the basic education in India, combined with what it calls the natural numerosity of the Indian mind, makes Bangalore unique and may not be readily reproducible in the other proposed cyber locations.

If one considers that there is approximately a 50-year gap between the dawn of the knowledge revolution in the USA and the emergence of the new economies of East Asia, that would to an extent explain the magnitude of the divide. However, because of the massive spread of computerisation in virtually every sphere of human activity, adaptation to new learning has turned out to be quite rapid. Thus a distinction needs to be made between the use and application of knowledge and generation and innovation of new knowledge. The competitive advantages of these two distinct skills remain to be explored fully.

4 Moving out of the Comfort Zone – the Role of Business

Introduction

The relationship between business managers and their counterparts in a firm's R&D laboratory has a fairly long history and is still an inconclusive debate. This is also true, to some extent, regarding the relationship between scientists in industry and their former research colleagues and mentors in the university, as well as their peer groups elsewhere. Although not much definitive and systematic research has been undertaken to understand the nature of these types of transactional relationships, nevertheless at least some qualitative understanding of such relationships is extremely important as they determine the effectiveness of R&D in industry and its impact on business performance. The nature of human relationships and interactions determines the quality, productivity and flow of knowledge across vast but somewhat amorphous networks, traversing business organisations, academia and other R&D institutions, which ultimately determine the innovation intensity in most businesses. Even in industries which trace their origins to some unique scientific discoveries or high-technology venture capital kick-starts, as these companies grow, there appears, in due course, a gradual drift between the business end and their R&D end. In most such organisations, with the passage of time the valuable lessons of corporate learning, to which the business owes its start-up and success, gradually become mystified and blurred. Throughout the 1970s, 80s and even the 90s, there are numerous examples of such business–R&D disjunctions, especially in the electronic, information technology and biotechnology industries.

Although the industrial R&D–academia relationships have a long history, the precise nature or pattern of their utility has remained fairly diffused. There are, of course, well-known examples of individual acad-

71

emics and certain universities who have developed strong and productive links with industry, but these are in the minority. Studies undertaken on the origins and success of places such as Silicon Valley in California, Route 128 in Massachusetts, and some of the more successful technology parks in Europe have failed to reveal any generic patterns which might define conditions which may have helped the relationships and linkages, and which could provide guidelines for others.

Funding of research projects in universities by industry is a fairly common and old practice, as indeed are generous, and sometimes business-related, philanthropic endowments to universities made by various industries and certain individuals. But here again, such relationships have primarily been like that between a vendor and a customer, and with notable exceptions the overall utility has tended to be obscure in terms of business or societal benefits. It is therefore worthwhile at least to explore the nature of academic relationships at the firm level as well as between business groups and the R&D department within a firm, in order to establish some sustainable and productive transactional patterns. Understanding such transactional relationships is likely to be highly rewarding in terms of effective innovation management in business, on the one hand, and turn out to be scientifically rewarding for the academic partners, on the other.

Business–R&D relations

In most sectors of the industry, there has traditionally been a subtle but somewhat adversarial relationship between business managers and their counterparts in R&D. While all successful businesses acknowledge the vital role of R&D as essentially a competitive investment, nevertheless there is a reasonably widely held view that the rewards from R&D are far less compared to the cost of undertaking R&D. Such internecine tensions, although widely prevalent, rarely surface in the public domain because of the highly price-sensitive nature of such corporate dissonance. The public posture is usually one of pride in a firm's commitment to R&D as a strong weapon in its armoury, as expressed by a progressively rising allocation of funds, especially during times of business upturn and periods of prosperity. A firm's R&D department's attitude and behaviour, on the other hand, are generally moulded by the awareness that its survival and well-being are dependent on funds to be allocated by the business, annually.

As a consequence of various developments which are currently clustered under the terms globalisation and knowledge explosion, traditional relationships between a firm's business and R&D managers are having to change radically, driven primarily by the competitive compulsions of the marketplace. It has now been established beyond doubt that businesses which have developed the competencies and skills continuously to update their knowledge about consumers and market forces, and are then able to convert such knowledge into goods and services, with the help of science and technology-driven innovations, invariably succeed in their pursuit of market leadership and dominance. The linkage of consumer knowledge to R&D via a firm's innovation process is the fundamental factor which is radically transforming the working relations between business managers and their colleagues in R&D. As has been mentioned elsewhere, since the half-life of innovations, in virtually every sphere of trade and commerce, is dropping dramatically, successful companies, typically, seek to achieve at least a third of their annual revenues from products and services which have been less than three years in the marketplace. Given such an intensity of change as well as its implications on the supply chain, marketing costs, and so on, business managers are compelled to ensure that their choice of funding market-driven R&D priorities has a very high chance of meeting target dates and cost milestones. Under such conditions, R&D managers are becoming more accountable *vis-à-vis* business performance.

A better understanding of the dynamic nature of markets, on the part of R&D managers, is enhanced by formal and continuous, task-related transactions with their business colleagues, eventually producing a set of mutually committed task covenants. R&D managers very quickly learn that no matter how scientifically exciting and successful a particular piece of discovery may be, if it does not relate to a clear business description of market opportunities, such discoveries are indeed of very little or no value to the firm. For example, it is reasonably common to hear fairly intelligent scientists complain how some of their original discoveries, if exploited by the business, could have changed the fortunes of the corporation. Such attitudes can be readily traced to the utter ignorance and remoteness of individual scientists from the realities of the marketplace. IBM and Philips are two contemporary and well-publicised examples of such attitudes. For this state of affairs, both the R&D as well as the business managers share the blame in equal measure. On the other hand,

when R&D and business managers work as partners, R&D management begin to appreciate that seeking annual funding from business is
far less important compared to defining jointly with business
managers corporate business opportunities, solving which, at the end,
are the real source of sustainable corporate profits and hence R&D
funding. When such market goal-driven, business–R&D transactions
become gradually formalised, there takes place a subtle cultural
change both in attitudes as well as in corporate behaviour, which is
both profound and enriching. Modern business leaders are differenti-
ated from their predecessors who funded R&D but remained perpetu-
ally dissatisfied with research outputs and unfulfilled promises, by
being more consultative, participative and more committed as stakeholders of their business R&D projects. Modern business managers
see R&D not in 'we and they' terms but more as a productive partnership to generate high rates of new innovations with which to win
battles in the marketplace.

Another important development is that, when innovation becomes
the driving force to change a business culture, business leaders realise
that innovative ideas and opportunities can and do arise from markets
and operations all around the world. For example, as a result of
advances in IT and telephony, some companies have set up formal
systems to capture, collate, screen and act upon each innovation idea,
from its various operations, with the help of the 'new innovation
ideas' information highway, linking all parts of the corporation on a
24-hour basis. This virtually continuous and real-time collection and
screening of ideas for new innovations requires specialised skills for
those responsible for co-ordinating this activity. In order to undertake
this activity, reliably and effectively, such individuals have to be
exposed to specialised training.

It must, by now, be apparent that such a complex transactional
process involving literally hundreds of employees across the firm,
also raises the accountability of business managers in terms of formulating precise business performance goals. In this new way of
working, business managers are now required not only to forecast
more precisely their business growth and profitability targets but also
have to underpin such targets with specific innovation, R&D and
marketing programmes. Thus it is no longer acceptable to explain
away, say, that profit targets were not met because of some unanticipated events in the market or that R&D had not delivered what it had
promised, as usual!

There are a number of other related developments which influence the new ways of working and target setting described above. Business managers now feel obliged to plan and undertake formal discussions with R&D managers, underpinned by marketplace and consumer data, for each innovation proposal, before any project work can commence. In addition, as discussed in Chapter 5, business and R&D managers jointly have to monitor progress of each innovation project periodically, since the performance of the business depends upon the success of these projects. This process of periodic but fairly formal and detailed interaction with R&D managers raises the awareness among business managers of the inherent uncertainties and the precise nature of risks associated with scientific exploration. Traditionally, businessmen tended to be bewildered and disappointed by delays and failures of R&D projects, being unaware of the degree of risks or the complexity inherent in the pursuit of scientific research. On the other hand, in this new paradigm, the normal tendency of research scientists to be over-optimistic is tempered by the realisation that targets have not only to be agreed but delivered as well.

During the transition from a 'we–they' culture to one of partnership, R&D personnel also undergo a number of different attitudinal shifts. In addition to becoming much more target conscious, the most important shift is from 'businessmen do not understand the profound and risky nature of creativity' to 'we all better work as a team to make the business succeed'. In between there are various shades of attitudes and feelings. For example, it has been observed that in a business where there is a steady and successful stream of innovations driving the business's growth and profits, business leaders readily appreciate the need for earmarking funds dedicated to high-risk exploratory and blue-sky research. Unfortunately, scientists are not always very pleased, even after receiving steady funding for basic research, when business managers wish periodically to review the status of exploratory science projects. Such reviews help business managers to comprehend whether the basic research projects continue to be of relevance for the long-term interests of their business. Many scientists consider such business enquiries as a form of uninformed intrusion into their domain; some even go to the extent of protesting that such scrutiny of their basic science research by the business could inhibit creativity. In my experience, I have found such resentful attitudes of scientists to questioning by business peers, as inhibiting creativity, could not be further from reality. In fact, such continuous interactions with business help to dispel the unnecessary aura of mystery and profundity commonly surrounding scientific research. In real-life experience, I have discovered that the majority of scientists, at a firm level, feel delighted, relieved and liberated in such a new environment of close and intimate working with business colleagues on well-defined business goals. The really competent scientist is able to balance the practical needs of the business without in any way diluting the rigour and commitment required to carry out leading-edge and basic scientific enquiry. It is the less capable and competent scientists who feel threatened in this new era of transparency and it is not too difficult to see why they feel the way they do. As far as creativity in science is concerned, a degree of accountability instils a desired sense of discipline in exploratory research; in its absence uncharted creativity mostly ends up in chaos.

Formalising the process

The proactive business-driven interaction with R&D, as described above, can only be sustainable and productive if it is conducted within a formal framework. The constituents of such formal frameworks include the conduct of business–R&D transaction, the assessment of risks of undertaking a certain line of exploration, and monitoring progress of project milestones. In terms of detail, some of these procedures may differ from one firm to another. For example, a firm which operates its business within a smaller geography may adopt a different procedure compared to, say, an MNC with widely dispersed global operations. However, there are some common procedures which, when applied uniformly, have been found to reinforce the business–R&D interactive process, irrespective of the size or scope of a firm's activities. For example, in this new dispensation, the annual business planning and prioritising meeting is, ideally, jointly chaired by the head of a business and the head of R&D along with their respective senior strategy and operations colleagues. The main impact of such joint meetings is the high visibility of business–R&D interaction. Second, everyone concerned with a particular business in the firm becomes fully aware of the strengths, weaknesses and vulnerabilities of a particular business, its critical R&D requirements as well as its innovation capabilities. The third important benefit is that decisions agreed at such joint meetings get to be owned at the highest level in the company. The outcome of such business-driven R&D meetings invariably includes choice of long, medium and short-term priorities, discontinuation of certain projects, the increase or paring of resources and assessment of progress of ongoing projects. Periodic reviews of progress also include topics such as performance of business against agreed objectives, along with delivery by R&D against agreed targets. Such full-scale business R&D reviews are typically undertaken two or three times a year. Since the seniormost managers from the business and R&D participate in these review meetings, preparation for these annual or biannual reviews and decision-making processes requires a great deal of homework and prior planning. Such prior preparation for business–R&D review meetings is separately undertaken by project-specific supply chain and R&D teams, dedicated to individual projects or scientific disciplines, as well as by joint marketing and R&D innovation project teams as may be appropriate. Thus the quality of homework and that of other pre-reading literature provides the foundation for the productive conduct of the above-mentioned business–R&D reviews and decision-making process.

As successive review meetings take place at periodic intervals, there is a rapid accumulation of learning, and some best practices on business–R&D planning begin to emerge in a firm. Naturally, such best practices can in turn be shared across business groups and R&D laboratories within a firm. The process veritably triggers off a chain reaction across the corporation and all its business subsidiaries. This business-driven R&D transactional process works because it is procedurally simple and transparent. Why such a simple idea has taken so long to take root in most businesses is a moot question. The historic, cultural and attitudinal divide between people engaged in scientific research or those making money was allowed to remain wide. Overcoming such differences has now become imperative to the successful conduct of business. This has meant that fundamentally business as well as R&D managers have had to step out of their traditional comfort zones.

Project team as an entity

What has been described up to now is a broad framework for a disciplined way of working in the management of business-driven R&D. Another major advantage of the interactive management process described in the previous section, is a formalised approach to the allo-cation of R&D resources to business priorities and sharpening of accountability for delivery and performance. One invariable conse-quence of working in such a formal process is that it normally throws up many more potentially attractive business ideas compared to the resources available within a firm, usually both in the business as well as in the R&D department. The process of deciding which ideas to take up for further exploration and which not to, is probably the most difficult exercise of all. Choices are forced by the availability of resources, and many exciting project proposals have, as a conse-quence, to be relegated to the back burner. The ultimate decisions are guided by the principle of LESS is MORE. In other words, if priority projects are selected based on probability of success, impact on profits, competitive factors and so on, and can be provided with adequate resources, there is a higher probability of success as opposed to trying to stretch available resources to cover as many attractive projects as possible.

The process of having to make difficult choices to match projects and resources, has been greatly facilitated by choosing to work in formal and dedicated *project teams*. The days when individual scientists worked in the isolation of their laboratories and suddenly came up with a brilliant discovery or a commercially attractive breakthrough are long over in industry. Individual scientists can still be found occasionally beavering away at some fundamental scientific problem. But this is becoming more and more an excep-tion nowadays in industry. Multidisciplinary teams, working on mega business-related scientific projects, are proving to be more productive, while also being cost-effective. Multidisciplinary teams of scientists, marketing managers, market researchers and so on create even more powerful combinations for high-profile innovation projects. The assembling and activation of such innov-ation teams or teams dedicated to fundamental science projects, is an intense and time-consuming exercise. Once activated such dedicated teams have been found to raise creativity, energy and output to levels which frequently surpass all expectations and prior experience.

The establishment of dedicated multidisciplinary project teams and management of large business-driven R&D projects is an emerging discipline. Of critical importance is training by specialists of teams in project management, team dynamics and risk assessment, as well as in developing team leadership and demarcating individual and collective accountability. A detailed description of how project teams are created and trained is given in Chapter 7.

Partnership with academia

In the previous section, I have described the traditionally variable and unstructured nature of the transactional relationships between business managers and their colleagues in industrial R&D. I then described how the introduction of some logical structuring and discipline in business–R&D interactions can be formalised and how such interactions can then turn out to be extremely rewarding and productive in terms of business performance. As a matter of fact, the transition from the old ways of working to some of the current best practices has become imperative for business survival and success.

In a similar context, it may not be entirely surprising that traditional relationships between industry and academia have remained amorphous. The issue therefore is how such relationships can be made more transparent, purposeful and sustainable. The subject of the industry–academia relationship has gained urgency because it is critical for sustaining a required degree of excellence in industrial R&D, while academia now urgently seeks new sources of funding to supplement its traditional resources. One positive fall-out from such mutual dependence is to reinforce the sustainability of industry–academia linkages.

Some of the reasons why industry's interest in academia has risen in recent times are obvious and reasonably well known (see Chapter 3). For instance, the pace of advancement of scientific research has been accelerating at a rate which makes it impossible for any single firm to have access to and manage a critical mass of science entirely on its own. As has already been emphasised, a firm's business strategy is the principal means to delineate its R&D priorities. In turn, the R&D priorities determine the quality and quantity of the R&D resource required as well as the shape of the corporate science base. The shape of such a science base helps to identify which areas of scientific research can be undertaken and sustained in-house and which areas need to be accessed externally. Arriving at a balance between the extent of basic scientific research which can be undertaken in-house and that which has to be outsourced, is becoming more and more critical because of two reasons. First, the results of the external work can have a very significant impact on the output of the firm's total R&D effort. Second, to exploit effectively the external R&D resources and results requires a certain level of in-house competence without which it is impossible to sustain partnerships. Formations for external research, as are currently being developed and practised, have, as a consequence, now become entirely different from the traditional project by project funding in universities by industrial R&D departments. There are a number of reasons why external scientific collaborations had to be modernised, some of which are described in the next section.

Traditional working relations

Although universities are the primary source for all entry-level scientific manpower recruited by industrial R&D laboratories, traditionally, the relation between universities and industry has been of an unspoken attitude of mutual caution. In the USA, however, examples of need-based relationships and collaboration between universities and industry can be traced to the early part of this century. Incidentally, such attitudes of caution between industry and academia, are not very different compared to the subtle attitude of mistrust between business managers and their R&D colleagues described earlier. University faculty and science researchers generally feel that they have committed themselves to some higher calling, and indeed a few of them do, dedicating their lives to the advancement of humankind through the exploration of nature. By undertaking this calling, they believe they have sacrificed the pecuniary rewards which could have been theirs for the asking, if they had strayed into industry or some other 'lesser' vocation. Scientists in industry, on the other hand, try to sustain a relationship with their former mentors and continue to seek the respect of their academic peer groups, by publishing some of their own scientific research and attending conferences and seminars, but above all by providing funds for research projects to their former professors and academic departments. It is however fair to state that, in the vast majority of instances, university projects funded by scientists in industry are generally of mutual interest to the firm and a particular academic department in question. But in many instances, once funds are allocated, they tend to become an annual affair, almost automatically renewed, year after year. Cases have been known where the quality of output and the utility of what was originally a very good initiative, gradually become obscure in utility and value to the business. There have been extreme instances where both the industrial scientist who had commenced funding a particular project and a particular professor who received such funds, had both in course of time moved on to other things, and for several years thereafter the 'project' continued to be funded by the industry in complete ignorance of the state of affairs at both ends. While this might be an extreme example, somewhat like the pension being continued to be despatched to a person who has long since died, unfortunately such instances are not as rare as one may wish they were. While in many industrial R&D units internal project management itself is rarely a strong and disciplined process, under such circumstances, it would be unusual that externally funded projects are likely to be more efficiently managed.

At this stage, it is worth digressing a bit to explain some traditional practices in industrial R&D units, which not only influenced their internal effectiveness, but also spilled over into management of external relationships. Historically, in the absence of a formal process of R&D management and administration, the best substitutes tended to be slight variations of a firm's accounting and auditing procedures, loosely adapted in R&D as management and control tools. In companies where such conditions still prevail, business-research discussions primarily focus on funding issues and annual plans are discussed in terms of units of costs and manpower numbers. Such R&D funding procedures should have, ideally, been assessed in terms of innovation intensity and achievements of milestones, of all science and technology projects and as they relate to business needs. To compound the shortcomings of how funding is planned, important management functions in R&D, such as human resources management or external project funding are frequently entrusted to older scientists, many of whom may have outlived their productive period in their scientific disciplines. The impact of poor human resource management in industrial R&D is discussed in Chapter 7. Similarly, many industrial laboratories tend to entrust the management and administration of externally funded research projects to people who themselves were probably not outstanding scientists to begin with, and who are quite prepared and happy to end their last working years as administrators of external research, usually with very little accountability for either costs or results. Many such individuals quite enjoy the attention they receive from their academic peers who benefit from such funding from industry, and also gain ready and welcome entry into academic corridors and bask in those uncomplicated surroundings. Considering that in some industries quite substantial sums are earmarked for externally funded research projects, such diffused accountability of their management, as has been described, is indeed mystifying. For instance, when an industrial R&D scientist sponsors a project with his former professor, arising, in most cases, from a genuine need, he finds it extremely difficult, if not impossible, to discontinue such projects and funding even after their utility may have come to an end. Although these observations are likely to raise a howl of protest from the community of industrial R&D managers, nevertheless the practices, as have been described above, are fairly widely prevalent in all the advanced industrialised nations and hence are worth highlighting.

During the 1990s, several well-known Japanese companies donated fairly large sums of funds to universities, particularly in the UK and on the east and west coasts of the USA, to set up centres for undertaking fundamental research in areas of their business interest. It is reasonably well known that in Japan itself Japanese universities did not, until relatively recently, undertake collaborative research with Japanese industries as is prevalent in the West. It is, of course, another matter that this has now begun to change in Japan as well, and Japanese universities now welcome funding and collaboration with both Japanese and foreign companies. Most research centres funded by Japanese firms in the West were set up on the basis of minimal business accountability on part of the university, but gave fairly free access to the Japanese managers and scientists of the investing firms to a particular university and its academic departments. Some research directors of Japanese firms which have provided such funds have, somewhat reluctantly, admitted the limited value of their major initiatives with Western universities to their company's business strategy. Considering the traditional commercial astuteness as well as the discreetness of the Japanese, such an admission is indeed surprising. Furthermore, of late, the funding commitments of many Japanese firms have also come under strain because of the severe economic recession in Japan. The subject that remains to be explored is that of managing externally funded projects over distances, and especially in instances which are compounded by problems of culture and language. The evolution of virtual networks to fund, monitor and manage outsourced projects and partnerships is of more recent origin and is discussed in Chapter 6.

Emerging patterns – partnership

Two key developments, in the academic world, are primarily responsible for the change of attitude in universities regarding R&D in industry. In the past quarter century, America became the pioneer in producing a new breed of academic scientist-entrepreneurs. Many successful American academic scientist-entrepreneurs are people of exceptional brilliance and creativity – many are Nobel Laureates. They exhibit a powerful common trait: the ability to commercially exploit their discoveries to create wealth for themselves as well as for society without sacrificing the very high quality of their scientific research. These entrepreneurs do not see any contradiction in being successfully creative and rich at the same time, unlike their equally illustrious predecessors who happily spent their time in sackcloth and ashes. The question of who came first – the entrepreneur-scientist or the venture capitalist – remains somewhat obscure. But since the early pioneering days, the venture capitalists, as a class, have had unusual catalytic influence in spreading the scientist-entrepreneur culture quite widely in the USA. Subsequently and quite naturally, some of these venture capitalists and their culture of spawning scientist-entrepreneurs has spread, first to the UK, and gradually to other parts of Europe, but as yet, far less effectively as compared to America.

The second event which has helped change the attitude of university scientists towards money is the growing shortage of funds traditionally available to universities, and particularly for academic research. Most nation states are finding it difficult to allocate the increasing amounts of funds demanded by their educational and research institutions. In almost all countries therefore, including recently even Japan, universities are being actively encouraged to search for alternative and additional sources of funds and become active players in the global free-market society. In this process, they are also being encouraged to help create more wealth with their knowledge. Unlike Europe, fundraising has been professionally managed in private American universities for a much longer time. The argument goes that since universities are the prime source to provide human resources to industry as future leaders, managers and other wealth creators, industry quite naturally should be an important source of funding for universities, in its own self-interest. As a consequence, there is emerging a fairly large element of branding and marketing in the recent academic fundraising strategies. Indeed, the quality of faculty, certain areas of unique specialism, the quality of the graduates, the illustriousness of the alumni, the reputation of the quality of scientific research and so on are all becoming a part of the unique selling proposition (USP) of a university in this new scenario. However, in Europe such an approach has not yet been organised with the attention to detail with which it is developing in the USA. As a consequence, management of fundraising has progressively become both complex and sophisticated, forcing many universities to employ full-time professional managers (some still designated deans!) dedicated to the collection of funds. Such a remarkable change in the attitude of academia towards money and wealth has coincided with industry's compulsion to seek closer links with key university research programmes and also raise the overall efficiency of funds allocated to outsourced research. As an aside, it must be mentioned that there are indeed those well-known exceptions of colleges and universities in the UK and Europe, whose considerable inherited wealth is so well managed as to be the envy of many professional fund managers. Therefore, wealthy institutions still consider seeking funds from industry somewhat beneath their dignity.

In many large firms the central function for administering externally funded research by former scientists, is also being disbanded as it is considered to be either unproductive or of doubtful utility. Some of the old central systems are being progressively replaced by different firm-specific management processes. One of the more widely used practices is a decentralised process in which industry R&D project groups or teams determine, in their project planning process, the nature and duration of external inputs required. They also specify departments or individual academics who meet such requirements as the case may be. For example, in case of a firm's megascience themes, it may become essential to create formal long-term partnerships with one or more academic departments. Such focused funding usually turns out to be highly productive and in many cases leads to establishment of very long-term partnership links between the firm and an individual or an academic department.

Since such academic partnerships have a direct impact on the success of the firm's business–R&D projects, all externally funded projects are subject to periodic review by R&D project leaders, somewhat similar to the review of the business projects referred to earlier. The debate regarding sharing of rewards from patents, which might result from such industry–academia collaborations, is an ongoing one. Sometimes this is used as an excuse to build walls between a firm and an academic department in question. Fortunately, in most cases firms have unambiguous policies regarding intellectual property which most universities consider fair and equitable. The degree of fairness is based upon the element of risk which the firm bears. There are other instances where the patent issue has to be resolved almost on a case-by-case basis with external partners. But in all instances, the patent clause has to be unambiguously built into any partnership contract, between a firm and an academic institution or an individual involved.

In the area of fundamental research, especially involving a mega-scientific topic, it is usually found to be worthwhile to enter into longer-term *partnerships* with more than one academic institution as well as more than one individual scientist, in order to generate a critical mass. The term *partnership* implies a sense of sharing as opposed to the historic donor–receiver relationship. In order to keep abreast of advances in different disciplines of science, of relevance to a firm, it has become necessary to put in place multidisciplinary teams of scientists to service different interdisciplinary megascience themes. The days of a lone scientist beavering away in isolation exploring some blue-sky problem and occasionally coming up with break-throughs are more or less over as far as industry is concerned. Once a science megatheme and its project team are in place, within a firm's R&D set-up, it then becomes possible to determine what external linkages may be needed for the megatheme, in order for it to achieve a critical mass and to remain at the leading edge of advances in that particular area of science. As discussions are initiated with potential partners in academia related to a firm's strategic megascience theme, this invariably leads to heightened interest in a particular university group which then becomes extremely keen to participate actively in such major initiatives. Although the response to project- or programme-based partnership with industry varies from individuals to individuals, generally the response is found to be most positive among the younger group of academic researchers. They also happen to be, without exception, individuals who have already achieved very high levels of scientific prominence, as a result of their personal or group research achievements.

There are some interesting reasons why a particular group of academic scientists feels attracted to partnerships with industry. First, although because of their research record and scientific achievements, such individual scientists receive independent research grants, they consider partnership with industry as a source to provide a better critical mass with a larger peer group, as well as a source of additional funds. But probably an even greater attraction for such academic scientists is that partnership with industry enables them to relate even their most fundamental scientific explorations to marketable end products or services. Thus being able to link a particular piece of fundamental exploratory research to a firm's long-term business strategy, is considered by young and successful academic scientists as being in tune with contemporary sentiments of accountability and social relevance. More often than not, as a consequence, a very eminent academic scientist will readily agree to join an industry R&D project team itself, either as a leader or as one of its members, as may be appropriate, rather than remain only an external expert advisor. Most universities nowadays, provide for their academic staff to devote anywhere between 10 per cent and 30 per cent of an individual's time to participate directly in large industry science programmes. Invariably such bright, young and eminent academic scientists, who thus become partners with industry, enrich the firm's R&D environment significantly. On their part, they also readily admit to a greater sense of satisfaction in experiencing how results of fundamental research help create wealth in society. The fear that is still expressed from time to time is that such a commerce-driven focus of fundamental scientific research may prevent chance discoveries from occurring or achieving the prominence they deserve. This feeling has not been borne out by facts. In absolute terms, more profound discoveries in physics, chemistry, biology, medicine and mathematics have been made in the last quarter century of this millennium than ever before, aided by the emergence of inter- and trans-disciplinarity in scientific efforts, by large and, in many instances, geographically dispersed teams of scientists. It has, of course, meant that both the academics as well as scientists in industry have had to step out of the comfort zone of their earlier donor–recipient relationships and participate in new formations of greater transparency and accountability.

More recently, a new source of partnership is emerging as a result of the explosive growth of specialist R&D boutiques, in areas as diverse as human genome, telephony and software research. Then there are others which provide specialist services for the mass-scale screening and testing of a wide variety of molecules and drug candidates. Industries are finding it both rejuvenating as well as cost-effective to link some of their core R&D facilities with these newly emerging venture capital units, either by partnering specific projects or through some other long-term equity-based partnership arrangements. This emerging concept of creating external networks of high-expertise partnerships is now spreading rapidly in the USA and will, in due course, be adopted in Europe and, may eventually, set the pattern for other industrialising countries. With the emergence of a number of such new opportunities, particularly in the last ten years, we are witnessing new patterns of enterpreneurship linking science with business, in ways which have never been witnessed before. The performance of the high-technology stocks in the NYSE signals profound and fundamental developments of business evolution, yet to be witnessed, beyond the performance of those companies which are listed.

Participative R&D issues

The discussion on R&D partnerships will not be complete without referring to issues related to companies participating in R&D programmes, sponsored by national governments. Most governments are keen for industry to participate and thus raise the productivity from state-funded science by advancing wealth creation and employment generation. This subject was briefly referred to in Chapter 2. The LINK programme of the Department of Trade and Industry of the UK government and the Framework Programmes (currently the 5th) of DGXII of the EU are two more prominent current European examples. These two programmes have been operating for some years and serve to illustrate some of the management issues involved. The LINK programme brings together both large industries and small and medium-sized enterprises (SMEs) along with relevant universities' academic departments to work on very large R&D programmes of interest to all the partners. Each such R&D programme has a dedicated co-ordinating manager, besides designated members from each participating party. Matching funds are provided by government and participants. Tasks, milestones and so on are reasonably well defined by the project co-ordination manager in consultation with the participants. LINK, which has been in existence for a few years, has successfully completed a number of such large R&D projects. The overall knowledge base in any particular R&D area has most certainly been advanced, more than might otherwise have been the case, as a result of the work done in most of the projects completed by LINK. But the overall impact on wealth creation and employment generation in the UK still remains somewhat obscure.

In addition, the ownership or sharing of intellectual property arising from such combined efforts in each of the LINK projects was not always able to be resolved satisfactorily. As a consequence, the real utility of many of these projects remained somewhat under-exploited. It must nevertheless be acknowledged that many of the ideas in the UK government's well-known Foresight Initiatives can be traced directly back to the experience gained in the LINK initiatives. LINK also helped to significantly enhance interaction between large, medium and small industries, along with universities and Research Councils in the UK, in ways which would not have been possible otherwise. The EU R&D Framework Programmes have similarly, and successfully, forged strong linkages between industry and academia all across Europe and generated several national and cross-national initiatives to advance the creation of wealth and generate employment with the help of science and technology. The UK and European experiences provide many common lessons and experiences and will no doubt make more advances.

Both the European and the UK programmes are endowed with large funds and provide attractive conditions for industry R&D labs to seek active participation. Managers of industry R&D laboratories find initiatives like LINK and EU Framework programmes as attractive sources to supplement their internal resources, and in this way help make their industrial R&D more cost effective. However, the ease of participation in such government-sponsored programmes, especially for firms of repute, should caution industry R&D managers very thoroughly to analyse and document the potential benefits to the firm and its business objectives from any such programme. Otherwise, participating in such national or international programmes, while looking attractive in terms of accessing additional external resources, and being in tune with the practice of creating external networks as well as contributing to a national initiative, may turn out to be dilutive of the core objectives of the firm. The whole subject of state-sponsored multiparty participative R&D projects and their real value and contribution have yet to be fully explored and understood in commercial terms. The management of such large projects and extracting real value, at the national level, from them also remains to be established. But that such initiatives can deliver certain benefits, both at the firm as well as the national level, must be beyond any doubt. At the firm level it is absolutely essential to define clearly the benefits from such large external participative activity. Without clarity, in business terms, such efforts may end up, at best, as a goodwill gesture. Being able more precisely to define benefits at a firm level, is the best way to extrapolate and assess advantages at a national level.

Summing up

The high level of uncertainty which has traditionally surrounded R&D in industry is now beginning to be dealt with in a variety of ways to reduce or even eliminate such uncertainties. The compulsions of globalisation of business, as well as other pressures of the competitive forces in diverse marketplaces, is forcing industry leaders to manage technology and innovation more purposefully. The traditional barriers and disjunctions between industrial R&D laboratories and business operations are rapidly disappearing under the pressures of new competitive challenges. Scientists in industry are expected, more than ever before, to keep up with the rapid advances in their area of specialism, while improving their understanding of the business goals, and then to seek ways to link science and the marketplace. Business managers now seek close working relationships with colleagues in R&D in order to drive innovation aggressively and fuel business growth. This joining of forces by business and R&D managers is bringing about a profound change both in business operation as well as how R&D is managed in any particular business.

In order to sustain a critical mass in any area of science of interest to a firm, it invariably needs to establish formal and well-managed partnerships with universities and eminent academics. Such partnerships and collaborations are being greatly facilitated by changing attitudes and conditions in universities and research institutions. The process of external collaboration is now advancing rapidly, in businesses, all across the developed world. Traditionally, Japanese universities had remained isolated from Japanese industry. But even in Japan, collaboration between the two is now more popular than was the case even five years ago.

Effective management of academic collaborations and partnerships is undergoing profound transformation at the firm level. It has been observed that clear, business goal-orientated R&D projects, including fundamental scientific research, now tend to be more sharply focused and therefore better managed. Such project-specific partnerships are increasingly preferred, both by industry and by academia, compared to the traditional funding and administrative practices. At the national level, governments are taking major initiatives to direct science and technology expenditure purposefully in order to create more wealth and generate more employment. The LINK programme in the UK and the EU's Framework programmes are intended to achieve such national goals by promoting R&D projects involving the participation of small, medium and large enterprises, universities and research institutions. While, undoubtedly, advantages are gained from such initiatives at the firm level, the management of such complex partnerships for more intense exploitation remains to be resolved fully. Managing such complex formations is uncomfortable, but is the only means to invest in science meaningfully and thus create wealth for a nation.

5 Innovation – Linking Science and Technology to Markets

Introduction

The aim of this chapter is to describe, in generic terms, how science and technology competencies and skills are built and managed in industrial R&D laboratories. Such a description will hopefully provide a background to issues such as the factors a firm may take into consideration in the choice of areas and funding of fundamental scientific research. Second, what are some of the more common mechanisms and methodologies which are used by firms to build their technological capabilities derived from investment in basic research? And finally, how does an array of such technological capabilities fuel the innovation engine of a company? In very rare instances, a firm embarks on R&D *de novo*. As has been described in Chapter 3, many if not most of the new high-technology companies in the USA trace their origins to one or more scientific discoveries in a university department or a venture capital funded company or a combination of the two. What distinguishes these companies is that the products which they bring to the market clearly fulfil some defined or unfulfilled consumer or customer demand. In the more traditional and large companies investments in R&D usually have a longer history. In their case, the R&D investments can usually be traced to initial business growth and diversification. Such chicken-and-egg differences between the old and the new are not really material other than the fact that the modern American high-technology companies are really the pioneers of the concept of business-driven R&D. The lessons from, and the way of working of, these new high-technology companies are important for large companies with big R&D laboratories and expenditure. But, as has been described in Chapter 7, the difficulties created by the Human Factor severely restrict the agility and responsiveness in large corporations.

The published literature on R&D is rich with descriptions of venture capital driven R&D compared to R&D in large companies. Therefore, much of the description in this chapter is about firms of the second type in which large investments are made over a long period in R&D. The second assumption is that most large industry R&D set-ups are a consequence of steady investments, both in fundamental as well as applied scientific research. It is usual in such R&D laboratories to find many good scientists, who have expanded their skills and competencies and taken charge in specific areas of the firm's technology base. Many such firms acknowledge that a constant stream of winning innovations are extremely important to sustain their good performance. Such companies are also aware of the critical role the shifts and changes in the knowledge universe (universities, research institutions, specialised agencies and so on) play, and the importance of this universe to sustain its science base and enhance the firm's risk taking capabilities. Creating and sustaining a vibrant and business-relevant R&D capability within an organisational ambience and culture is not difficult, but needs a degree of dedication and commitment in order for science, technology and innovation to become powerful tools in the armoury of business leaders. The aim of this chapter is to trace the knowledge chain linking universities with industrial R&D and industrial R&D with the marketplace via operating companies.

Technology, research and development

Some semantic problems

The terms 'technology', 'research' and 'development' are frequently used interchangeably, to convey information and describe issues, in day-to-day corporate and business transactions. The purpose for which these terms are used may serve the objective of communication reasonably well. However, the meanings get obscure and fuzzy when these terms are made use of by bureaucrats or national governments to formulate R&D policies while using the term 'R&D' to express economic views. Since science is the bedrock for wealth creation, any misunderstanding or misinterpretation of its vast and all-pervading influence can and does lead to disproportionate consequences. Frequently politicians, for example, are known to declare that an investment in a certain R&D scheme would lead to wealth creation and employment generation. In most cases, they do not have the vaguest idea how this is likely to happen. Acts of faith are not always necessarily a virtue.

Even in this day and age, policy makers as well as the lay public tend to classify industry into high-technology, low-technology or no-technology groups. Such classifications are both erroneous and misleading. In a vast majority of countries, national policies are based on such erroneous classifications and there are many glaring examples of the consequences of such policies. These include loss of growth opportunities, retarded economic development, and reduced employment generation – to cite a few obvious ones. The question is, if these are indeed such obviously erroneous concepts, why are such classifications still made use of? One answer could be because such over-simplified classifications of what are essentially very complex concepts may sit comfortably in the minds of the uninitiated. Thus the mental picture of high technology would normally include large chemical complexes, nuclear power generation, advances in medicine, space exploration and so on – activities which bedazzle the popular imagination. Low technology would generally embrace most of the service sector in the minds of the common man, such as the food and drink industry, banking, transportation and so on, while the rest of the economic activities where the interaction between man and machine is not visible, tends to be considered as having no technology of any consequence, such as travel, tourism and sports. In spite of the fact that today technology dominates every facet of human enterprise, the misconceptions regarding science and technology persist. One of the aims of this book is to demystify science and technology, at least in the context of business operations. Let us begin with some reasonable working definition. Take technology, to start with. *Technology may be defined as the vehicle or the means which enables scientific discoveries to be converted into goods and services.*

For example, when a new molecule of great potential importance is discovered by the R&D department of a pharmaceutical company and when the molecule has passed through the usual regulatory and testing regime and so on, the means needed to produce it in quantities for testing and eventual commercialisation usually require a combination of new and proven processes. The transition from discovery to a usable state is linked by technologies dedicated to the commercial exploitation of the molecule. It may be obvious, from this simple example, that not all new scientific discoveries or even most would necessarily need new technologies for their scale-up and commercial exploitation. It is the choice of a combination of appropriate processes, routes and methodologies which makes a specific technology unique for the commercialisation of a new discovery.

Research has been broadly defined as the orderly approach to the exploration of new knowledge. The objective of research is to advance knowledge and understanding for humankind, and the boundaries of the search are therefore limitless. Traditionally, a distinction is sought to be made between academic scientific research and industrial research. The former is seen to be unconstrained by boundary conditions, in contrast to the latter, where research in industry is more directed and better defined. In the past 25 years, these distinctions have begun to blur because the generation of *new knowledge* happens to be the common driving force for all scientific research undertaken anywhere. While no industry can sustain its scientific competencies without funding some amount of fundamental or blue-sky research, academic research is now more inclined to explore avenues for the application of the new knowledge they generate, mainly to be able to afford the cost of sustaining a critical mass of fundamental research. Because of the galloping advances in science and the increasing importance of inter- and trans-disciplinarity as well as team working to solve large and complex problems, suitable partnerships between academia and industry have become invaluable. Such partnerships are now also facilitated by the pressures of high costs of conducting leading-edge scientific research and the need to share resources in more non-traditional ways. As a consequence, university departments now warmly welcome proposals for partnership from industry more than ever before. This development is in stark contrast to the traditional funding of specific projects in university departments by industry. The establishment and management of partnerships with universities is also a new discipline where the human factor plays a very important role for the outputs to be productive and meaningful (see Chapters 4 and 7).

The distinction between *research* and *development* usually tends to become blurred when one tries to seek precise definitions for each of them. In the general case, *development can be described as the process by which knowledge emanating from scientific research is enabled to deliver goods or services, by using the vehicle of appropriate technology.*

These definitions of technology, research and development provide a means to comprehend the importance of their individual roles, as well as how they may interact holistically. Such definitions also underscore the fallacy of classifying industry into high-technology, low-technology and no-technology groups, which many still tend to do. All successful industries create wealth by the application of knowledge. R&D happens to be a principal source of new knowledge.

The confusion between the high- low- and no-technology classifications described above, also extends to the definition of R&D in industry. Such distinctions which are to a large extent artificial, have been described by Roussel *et al.* in their book *The Third Generation R&D*,[14] some of which was briefly referred to in Chapter 2.

Incremental R&D: small 'r' and big 'D'

The goal of incremental R&D is small advances in technology, typically based on an established foundation of scientific and engineering knowledge. The task is therefore not the technically risky one of uncovering and applying new knowledge but the expert applications of existing knowledge.

A typical example of incremental R&D is work on exploration and enhancement of efficiency of the supply chain. Particularly in a manufacturing module, large savings can be achieved by small and incremental improvements. But this definition represents only a small and partial view of R&D.

Radical R&D: large 'R' and often large 'D'

Radical R&D draws on a foundation of existing scientific and engineering knowledge but which alone is insufficient to arrive at the desired results. Additional scientific work has to be undertaken towards discovery of new knowledge with the explicit purpose of achieving specific objectives. For example, in applying a well-known biochemical pathway to explore the mechanism of action of a newly discovered molecule, it may become necessary to work on some related but heretofore unknown reaction mechanism which is integral to the new molecule. By its very nature, such explorations usually involve substantial technical risk, cost and time. While Roussel *et al.* (1991, p. xi)[14] claim that

> there is never certainty that R&D will get – in a practical cost-effective way – all the technical success for commercial success

this need not necessarily be an inherent weakness of radical R&D. While discovering new knowledge is inherently risky, success depends on the quality of risk assessment as well as very sharp definitions of goals and objectives. Successful companies stand out because they successfully manage radical R&D projects.

Fundamental R&D: large 'R' and no 'D'

A condition under which a company dedicates all its resources to blue-sky exploratory work and none to development capability worth mentioning, does not exist in industry. Therefore, whether fundamental, stand-alone 'R' exists anywhere outside academia or a few venture firms, is doubtful.

The ultimate shape and size of a company's R&D department poses a challenge of choice. The allocation of resources to basic research, developing technologies and managing innovation, typically over a period, acquires a format suitable for a particular firm. But the mix between the three elements will always remain dynamic, with the balance fine-tuned all the time to reflect the needs of a business.

The changing scenario

The way scientific research, both in academia and industry, has been transformed in the last 50–60 years is truly remarkable. To the layperson, the romance and excitement of Alexander Fleming's discovery of penicillin was matched by mysteries and legends of the Manhattan project. If scientists and engineers were left alone with sufficient funds, they could help nations win wars, conquer outer space and even dominate trade and commerce. People would readily point out that these were indeed the origins of modern electronics, genetics and aviation.

The changes to science and scientists as we know today, really began in the 1970s with the energy crisis and the inability of technology to provide some immediate comfort especially to energy over-dependent societies. Public disappointment was reinforced when science and technology were seen to have failed to provide answers to some of the new problems facing humankind, such as changes in the global climate and some dramatic new diseases such as AIDS and CJD or mad cow disease, to cite just a few. Of late, an undercurrent of new fear is building regarding the consequences of the advances in agricultural, animal and human genetics. The benefits to society through genetics are probably less well understood today compared to the fears that misuse of this knowledge may result in.

There is a second element which is probably not related to what has been described in the previous paragraph. In the past 10–15 years, governments around the world have had to reduce allocation to defence research as well as academic research in order to balance at least partially the social needs for health and welfare. On the other hand, industry in general is having to deal with increased competitive pressures and the realisation that its science and technology competencies can only be sustained in partnership with universities.

Simultaneously, while such transitions in the R&D environment are taking place, many of the old ways of working and managing the R&D process are also undergoing radical shifts and changes. Thus the old adage that spectacular discoveries will somehow happen and will then be exploited to create wealth stands discredited, and has been replaced by planning for big discoveries driven by fairly well laid out business and wealth creation goals. Accidental discoveries do still occur all the time. But people who are capable of grabbing hold of them have always been rare. It is only the specially developed and trained mind that is able to grab hold of the unexpected in scientific exploration and relate it to either a pool of knowledge or even an unrelated business need.

All this has meant that old style, geographically isolated R&D laboratories of big industries have had to get closer to large agglomerates and behave as *borderless R&D resources*. Such borderless R&D formations have, in turn, found it easier to integrate with businesses, on the one hand, and manage meaningful networks of partnerships with academics, on the other. Increasingly, companies are seeking to organise their R&D in ways which break the isolation of R&D from the rest of the company, in order to promote a culture which fosters task-driven partnerships between R&D managers and their counter-parts who manage business. Such radical changes in management philosophy and attitudes have been facilitated primarily by the advances in information technology.

Scientific research in industry

The quality and scope of fundamental scientific research in major industries tend to be on a par with leading universities and institutions. However, this is where the similarities end. Interdisciplinarity and intradisciplinarity are the hallmark of most of the basic scientific research undertaken in industry. The origins of inter- and intradiscipli-nary science can be traced to large state-funded projects during and soon after World War II. Not long afterwards, many physical scientists and some mathematicians became interested in the emergent excite-ment of biological discoveries. As a matter of fact, some of the major advances in biochemistry, biophysics, genetics, biotechnology and medical sciences were achieved as a result of breaking the fences surrounding the traditional organisations of chemistry, physics and biology. While in universities such initiatives resided primarily with individual senior scientists and their groups, inter- and intradiscipli-narity progressively became the guiding organisational focus in industry. In reality the increase in the innovation intensity of industrial goods and services began to increase at such a rate that in order to achieve ground-breaking advances it required multipronged scientific approaches. It is this process of change that helped the rise of inter- and intradisciplinarity. Such a change has, however, not diminished the importance of traditional disciplines such as classical microbiology, organic synthesis, natural products and so on, in different industries.

The creation of clusters of inter- and intradisciplinary scientific themes and the emergence of specialist groups working on such themes is an evolutionary process which is marked by constant reviews and reorganisation depending on the relevance of such clus-ters to specific business goals and objectives. Thus a large trans-disci-plinary basic science cluster in, say, organic synthesis may include enzyme biochemistry, microbiology, mathematical modelling and even genetic engineering. In large industrial organisations such permu-tations become feasible because of the diversity of in-house scientific talent available, supplemented, as required, by long-term partnership arrangements with university departments and other private and public research institutions. However, it is the responsibility of senior R&D managers and experienced scientists in industry to ensure that during such need-driven evolution of multidisciplinarity, the core competencies in science clusters are not only maintained but are also continuously upgraded to retain leading-edge capabilities in an industrial R&D laboratory. It is usual for large industrial R&D units actively to maintain, at any point in time, a large number of science clusters to generate a continuous stream of discoveries needed to feed the business relevant technology clusters. Technology clusters are the application entities or the usable vehicles which drive business innovation projects. How this takes place in practice is discussed in more detail in the following section. The satellite or supporting disciplines in science such as mathematics, statistics, combinatorial chemistry or biology and analytical sciences have to be maintained at standards required for the exploration of fundamental research problems. For example, advances in analytical sciences have been so spectacular in the past decade that, in addition to providing traditional means to analyse and interpret experimental data, some of the advanced techniques have become indispensable tools in the progress of scientific discovery itself. Thus atomic force spectroscopy or magnetic imaging spectroscopy are now indispensable for exploration at the atomic or even at *sub-atomic* levels.

The recent announcement of Perkin Elmer Corporation that it was promoting a mega project to unravel the human genome, under the leadership of Craig Ventner, is worth mentioning.[39] Perkin Elmer's origins are in the business of analytical spectroscopy instrumentation. Apparently, their analytical capabilities have achieved such uniqueness that Perkin Elmer have leveraged their business competence by joining the race to unravel the human genome completely in a dramatically shorter period of time in competition with other players in the field. The race to leverage unique scientific competencies to attack large and complex problems, and then race competitively ahead in business, is thus becoming a stark reality.

In this context the debate[2] whether a firm needs big 'R' and big 'D' or small 'r' and big 'D' or only 'D' is becoming somewhat redundant. Firms which decide not to undertake any in-house scientific research and are totally dependent on an external knowledge source to maintain their development competencies are likely to face limits to growth sooner or later. It is extremely difficult for any firm, without an adequate research base, to develop and sustain a level of management competence which would enable it to shop around and select scientific know-how, needed to advance the firm's development goals. Even if such a firm is able to establish partnerships with university scientists their ability to create meaningful science clusters, entirely from such relationships, would be severely limited. Second, managers of external science in firms with only developmental departments soon find themselves to be out of date and unable to deal with the external world of science. However, the size of the 'R' is absolutely firm specific. Some of the best contemporary examples are to be found in pharmaceutical companies where the rapidly rising costs of discovering new molecules are forcing many of these companies to seek strategic external partners. Many or most of new research techniques and specialisms are being developed faster by small specialist firms and venture capital boutiques. These small specialist companies offer a vast cafeteria of products and competencies which, collectively, are getting beyond the scope of any single large pharmaceutical company to generate in-house. Therefore, in the evolution of new science clusters in pharmaceutical companies, strategic partnerships or other forms of contractual arrangements with specialist boutiques are progressing faster than in most other businesses. Similarly, in the recent spate of M&As in the pharmaceutical industry one of the deciding factors is the synergy and cost-effectiveness of science clusters which can be created by such mergers.[42]

The importance of sustaining an appropriate level of in-house scientific capability at a firm level cannot be over-emphasised. Because it has now become imperative for all companies to seek outside alliances to sustain the required critical mass of inter- and intradisciplinary science clusters the issues related to the sharing of rewards from the emerging intellectual property rights has become a veritable land-mine. Not surprisingly, there has not emerged any unified basis as how best to deal with the subject. Even traditional patent specialists are not fully equipped to deal with sharing of rewards, between partners of diverse interests, of intellectual property rights. For the time being, these have to be dealt with on a case-by-case basis. The guiding principle in establishing long-term science partnership is that it has to be fair and equitable to the parties concerned in order for such partnerships to be productive and sustainable. These conditions are clearly enshrined in partnership covenants and usually with the proviso that such arrangements need to be reviewed periodically due to the inherent uncertainties surrounding the outcome from fundamental scientific explorations.

The ratio of funding allocated to fundamental research compared to technology development and near-term innovation projects varies between industry types and even between firms in the same industry. Each firm arrives at some optimum ratios and usually with the flexibility to adjust the ratios from time to time depending on business needs or exigencies. In most large and successful firms there is usually a core funding for the science clusters which is reasonably well protected in the medium to long term. Such funding is usually determined by the chief of R&D and in agreement with the CEO, but following a fairly detailed review with appropriate business heads of each basic science cluster and its longer-term relevance to a firm's particular business. While arriving at such decisions on the composition and cost of sustaining basic research clusters, the ultimate onus of the responsibility rests with the chief of R&D and his senior scientists. This responsibility arises out of, first, the large element of uncertainty surrounding the very nature of basic research and, second, the need to demystify the scientific issues so that their choices make sense in business terms. Therefore, the periodic review between R&D and business, of the basic research clusters, is not intended to question the wisdom of choosing and sustaining a set of fundamental science projects for a firm, but for all concerned to reassure themselves that the science choices continue to have a business validity and also to ensure that no new opportunities of relevance to the firm, are being missed.

Thus business–R&D reviews of fundamental research projects measure the effectiveness of the science clusters and their continued relevance to the technology competencies of the firm. The technology competencies are critical because they are one of the principal drivers of a firm's innovation programmes. In addition, in most firms the quality of science clusters are also judged by other measures such as patents, publications, citation indices, recognition/awards, share in government grants, and also by periodic external peer reviews.

The ability to maintain and manage a dynamic and leading-edge set of science clusters at a firm level is highly demanding and managerially complex as well. Dedicated project teams working on large inter- and intradisciplinary fundamental science projects have found the experience to be extremely rewarding and productive, especially when the outputs are related to business goals. One of the special features of project teams dedicated to fundamental research is that team members may be made up of both internal as well as external participants from universities and research institutions. As has been mentioned earlier, the external participants are attracted by the goal-orientated culture, even in basic research, in some business organisations. In certain instances the reputation of some scientists in a firm happens to be very high and many academic participants express keenness to join teams with such scientists in industry. Equally, it is not unusual for business science projects to attract very eminent academics to head industry science teams as team leaders. In such participatory relationships, university professors may spend 10–30 per cent of their time working in an industry unit. While physical proximity of industry R&D laboratories to particular universities does facilitate team working as described above, electronic networks have now reduced the importance of geographic proximity or cultural affinity.

The debate whether a firm should invest in one or more large central R&D facilities, or whether such facilities should be dispersed across the geography of a corporation, is an ongoing one. It is frequently a firm's operating companies which are the most keen to own R&D facilities within their geographical proximity. Usually, the profits of the operating companies are subjected to some central R&D cess. Also, the operating companies' chairmen's traditional inability to relate the central R&D cess to the central R&D units' benefit to the operating companies' performance leads to strained relations between central R&D and operating companies. The clamour for decentralisation has intensified with the advancement of electronic commerce which is rightly seen as a great facilitator. The argument against dispersed multilocation is not very strong. However, large central laboratories provide the ideal set-up to create a productive critical mass for undertaking fundamental research while also generating synergy because of inter- and intradisciplinary proximity. Whether similar critical mass and synergy can be achieved exclusively by electronically networked dispersed locations is not known at the present time. Thus, until more experimentation is undertaken on the utility, productivity and cost-benefit for the dispersal of basic scientific research in industry, the subject has to be dealt with due caution. However, the arguments in favour of dispersal of development and innovation resources to operating companies and then linking them by IT networks with central research are now overwhelming.

In most countries, industry is encouraged to invest in R&D by providing attractive tax and other incentives. Business sometimes gets sucked into investing in R&D as a tax-planning device. There are many examples of such tax planning and some other cost benefits which persuaded firms to disaggregate and disperse central R&D facilities. Usually such actions have tended to erode severely a company's science base. This represents an extreme case of questionable business relevance with a very short time horizon.

Much of the confusion and misunderstandings regarding the size and shape of investment that a firm may make in basic research arises because the distinction between fundamental scientific research and leading-edge development is not widely understood. This is compounded by the long-term nature and high risk inherent in basic research. Such long-term issues do not fit the pressures and realities of quarterly results. Frequently, in the hothouse environment of diverse business pressures, fundamental scientific research is seen as esoteric and of questionable utility. The only way to overcome such practical problems is for R&D and business managers to be able clearly to communicate the value of basic science projects as they relate to the business goals and objectives. Often problems of relating basic research to business goals arise because scientists, by training and temperament, do not like to be questioned by people outside their peer group. So it is not surprising, even in industrial R&D, that one often hears the refrain that frequent questioning and review of fundamental science projects by business colleagues dampens creativity. This indeed would be a serious impediment to the progress of research if it were true. But in actual practice it has been found that basic science projects which are sponsored, owned and nurtured jointly by scientists and their business colleagues enhance the utility of creative ideas. In any case, really good scientists possess sufficient self-esteem not to be offended by questioning by those who after all provide the funds for their research and also happen to be the customers of their results. Even academic scientists who become team members of business-science projects, find the review and assessment of research programmes by businessmen extremely worthwhile because it provides a commercial and value creation dimension.

An industry invests in fundamental scientific research in order to provide the base from which to build competitive benefits. Incidentally, this investment in science also helps to create an interface with the academic world. The interface assists in the attracting and recruitment of outstanding talent into industry as they emerge from academia. It so happens that the majority of new research recruits into industry commence their career in industry in one of its R&D laboratories. Furthermore, their initial assignment is usually in one of the basic research projects. It is thus interesting to note how many important roles basic research performs in industry.

In conclusion, fundamental scientific research is indispensable in the creation of a strong and productive industrial R&D edifice. Besides being a prime source of new knowledge and high quality human resource, investment in fundamental science ensures a sustained level of competitive capability. Business must never invest in science as an act of faith but rather as an act of strategic intent. The only way to achieve this objective, is by investing in scientific topics which are transparently linked to innovation programmes and business objectives of a company.

Under the catch-all of corporate re-engineering, any temptation to disaggregate or decentralise a company's central scientific resources, must be balanced by the knowledge that meaningful scientific competencies are built over a long period of time. Such a set-up cannot be dismantled-assembled-dismantled, at will. At the same time, closing down some well-entrenched scientific activities, which have outlived their utility or relevance, has to be done with care and determination. Investing in science to create knowledge and wealth is a very long-term commitment. It should not be undertaken in haste nor lightly discarded.

Technology and development

Technology and development are frequently and mistakenly used interchangeably. Technology can be defined in a number of ways. But in relation to scientific research, and in keeping with the theme of business-driven R&D, technology is the visible instrument with which to convert the outputs of basic scientific results in order to drive product and process innovations. Development, in contrast, is the process by which known or modified existing technologies are applied in order to improve existing products and processes. New technology normally evolves adjacent to where scientific research is taking place while development primarily takes place in dispersed locations. Most operating companies in firms run a development department of a size and with a range of activity commensurate with its business operations. Such development departments are usually managed by engineers and former scientists, and are normally located adjacent to manufacturing departments. It is usually the development department which links the marketing and manufacturing departments in an operating company. Being close to marketing, manufacturing and the marketplace, development departments, in operating companies, are ideally placed to undertake product and process modifications speedily to the benefit of the operating company bottom line. They are thus naturally highly valued by their manufacturing and marketing colleagues. In most operating companies, the development departments also maintain close working links with central R&D bound by shared projects, contacts and relationships built over years. These are over and above the project contacts with central R&D which are usually for large business projects. As has been mentioned earlier, operating company chairpersons are more comfortable with the proximity to their development departments because they are able to 'control' both costs and value of outputs as these relate to their own business. It is in comparison to development that a company chairperson questions both the cost and effectiveness of corporate R&D to his or her own company's performance. Both the attitude of the operating company chairpersons as well as the traditional role of development departments are undergoing changes. There are two primary reasons for these changes. One is that operating companies, corporate centres and R&D departments are beginning to be strongly linked together by common performance targets. The second is that new innovation processes and IT provide the glue which holds them in place in a seamless pattern (see Chapter 6). Even while these new formations are evolving, the traditional role of the company development departments for product and process and cost improvement need to be preserved, or even strengthened, because they fall outside the activities of the new innovations management process, while continuing to contribute to an operating company's short-term profits. Over a period of time, development departments become strong components of the innovation management process.

From this brief description of the role and function of the development department, the distinction between development and technology is probably clearer. In a company R&D unit, technology clusters emerge as more or less mirror images of the science clusters, which are described in the previous section. For example, a science cluster made up of microbial genetic, genetic engineering, monoclonal research, antigen–antibody reactions, enzymes and enzymology and so on could be linked to a corresponding biological material technology cluster consisting of fermentation methods, separation engineering, scale-up chemical engineering, biomass balance and so on. Thus a technology cluster would have the capability to validate the relevant and successful results of a science project and, if necessary, to undertake commercial viability assessment and other scale-up engineering tasks which may be required to drive an important innovation project for the company. In terms of an input–output matrix, technology clusters span across basic science projects and into innovation projects. This description, of course, does not necessarily mean that a particular technology cluster is solely dedicated to one science cluster. It is more usual than not that a technology cluster is enriched by results from science projects belonging to more than one science cluster, as may be the case. Individual technology projects, in many instances, may be linked in a network with outside institutions for inputs of science results which do not reside in the firm's own science base. Engineering is a third element in a technology cluster. More often than not successful new technologies require plant, equipment and processes, which are entirely novel. These have to be evaluated in terms of engineering and commercial feasibility early on.

The management of technology clusters and projects is thus quite distinct from the traditional development function and it is important not to mix these up. The management of technology projects follows the same disciplines of team and project management described in the next section. The individuals who work in technology clusters have typically spent time working and earning a reputation in basic research or are research engineers or belong to some other technical specialism. The leaders of technology clusters are invariably very successful former scientists who would usually have worked for several years in science clusters and grown familiar with other business processes as well during this period. Many such experienced scientists move to operating companies as directors of innovation centres. Managing such technology projects requires a combination of a record of performance in a particular discipline of science or engineering and management skill and competency to lead large multidisciplinary project teams. Such combinations provide unique opportunities to capable individuals to acquire new skills in the management of technology and technologists. Some of them turn out to be outstanding general managers and a few CEOs.

Innovation – concepts and process

The process of innovation and its management is one of the most important elements in companies which pursue the principles of business-driven R&D. A formal innovation process is able to weave all activities of a corporation, which other, more traditional company operations are no longer able to. A new innovation culture gets ready acceptance from all parts of a corporation because of innovation's powerful impact on profits and growth. Traditionally, the financial press have reported the R&D budgets of companies as one of the indices related to investing in the future. Financial analysts and shareholders consider such information as an indicator of the long-term health of a corporation. However, both inside a corporation as well as among interested external observers, the R&D budget alone is no longer a sufficient marker to the future of a company. R&D spending is now beginning to be more and more supplemented by indicators which measure the innovation intensity of a company. Innovation intensity is measured and reported variously by different companies. Some sort of standardisation and uniformity in publishing the innovation intensity will hopefully emerge in due course or may be promoted by the evolving standards of corporate governance. New product launches, product relaunches, operating margins, market share, brand leadership ranking and so on, are each indirect indicators of a company's innovation intensity. But none of them individually or together serve as an accurate indicator. Broadly, the innovation intensity of a company may be defined as 'the ratio of earnings from products which are not more than "x" years in the market to the total earnings of the company'. Thus, the higher the ratio, the greater the innovation intensity. Innovation is the prime instrument to leverage the knowledge emerging from R&D and to blend it with the knowledge gathered from the marketplace, in order to create superior goods and services produced and sold by a company.

The distinction between freewheeling and individually inspired innovation, on the one hand, and formal innovation processes managed by a team of professional specialists, on the other, is distinct but not entirely different. The former is a matter of individual propensity to innovate and innate ability to seek out original ideas and thoughts, while the latter is a much more deliberate management process to seek out business-relevant ideas and then convert them with the help of a series of well-charted steps into successful goods and services. This is in no way to underestimate the role of individuals in generating new innovative ideas, but rather to distinguish it from the systematic and successful exploitation of innovative ideas in discrete steps. The formal management of innovation has been described in detail by Wheelright and Clark[40] and provides much of the basis for the description that follows.

The basic steps in the formal innovation management process find wider application even in fundamental scientific projects as well as in technology projects discussed in the previous sections in this chapter. What is proposed to be discussed in this section pertains specifically to business-driven innovation projects aimed directly at the market-place. While basic science projects and technology projects are more or less exclusively managed by either dedicated teams of scientists or technologists, as the case may be, in contrast, business-innovation projects are managed by multidisciplinary project teams with members drawn from marketing, market research, development, R&D and so on.

Figure 5.1 outlines the 'skeleton' of building blocks which make up an innovation process, and in which the business strategy is the starting point. The largest number of books and articles on business is devoted to different aspects of business strategy and it is not my inten-tion to retrace this well-trodden ground. Suffice it to state that any business strategy is a dynamic concept, which is constantly influenced by competitive realities and a continuous feedback from consumers and markets upon which a business thrives. A business's strategy is the principal source of devising its R&D strategy. As has been described earlier, the R&D strategy then provides the means for building the science and technology base for a particular business, or more often a group of businesses. The business's innovation ideas are then converted into end products and services via the firm's science and technology base. The process by which innovation is managed is proposed to be described in some further detail. Finally, that new and successful innovations have to be continuously woven into a business's supply chain naturally goes without saying.

Wheelright and Clark[41] have proposed a visual method for dealing with new innovations and ideas and have described it with the help of the *innovation funnel* (Figure 5.2). The innovation funnel, which has been fairly widely used in many other texts to describe the process visually, provides an excellent basis to represent, monitor and manage innovation in business.

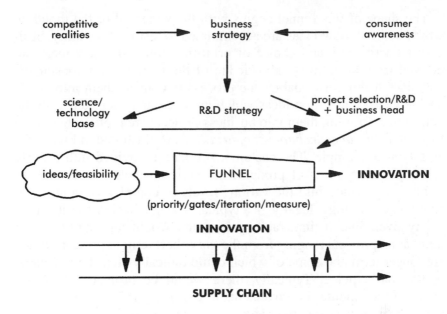

Figure 5.1   Building blocks in an innovation process

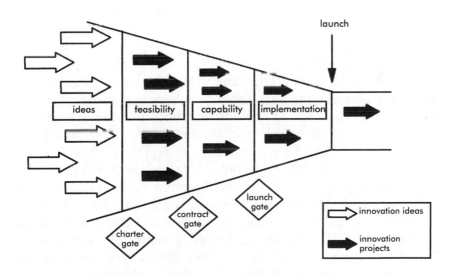

Figure 5.2   Components of the innovation funnel

The shape of this funnel begins with the wide-end or the mouth at which point all new ideas are accumulated to test for feasibility, business attractiveness and choice of priorities. Since the new ideas are derived from an intimate knowledge of the markets and consumers, and since technology enables the process to convert them into goods and services, innovation ideas which are eventually selected with the aim of transforming them into business projects are represented in the form of a *consumer/technology matrix*. This is illustrated in Figure 5.3 as a typical example. The customer ordinate is divided into a fairly self-explanatory class of products or services, while the technology ordinate is divided into the various levels of complexity in terms of enabling technology. Ideally, in a typical strategic business unit (SBU) at any given time, its innovation programme would consist of a mix of innovation projects ranging from the very short term to projects which are longer term and some of which could radically alter the end game in the marketplace. Typically, there would be projects which are aimed at incremental improvements to existing goods or services and would be expected to deliver ideally between one or at most two years from start. Creating new variants or smaller variations would form the next category of projects and would have a lifespan to completion of, say, between 15–30 months. Since these are somewhat derivative in nature, they are classified as *derivative*. *Platform* projects represent the next higher degree of change through fairly major technological intervention, derived from a flow of new scientific discoveries, relevant to a particular product or service. They eventually emerge as new end-products or services. Typically, they emerge as end-products in 30–48 months from commencement of the innovation. *Breakthrough* projects tend to be rare opportunities which are exploited from radical scientific discoveries. As already mentioned, these are groundbreaking and change markets and consumer perceptions in unprecedented ways. By their very description, such projects have very long gestation periods, usually in the order of five years or more.

The risk elements in each of these projects relate inversely to the gestation period. All innovation projects which a business decides to invest in are subject to systematic risk analysis and assessment (Chapter 8). Thus, the C/T (customer/technology) matrix provides a visual display and summary of a business's innovation programme. Each individual project is managed by formal and dedicated business-innovation teams and their progress is monitored individually. From the description so far it may have become apparent that for a particular innov-

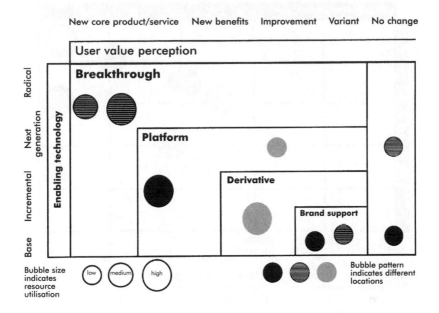

Figure 5.3 Customer/technology (C/T) matrix

ation project to find a place in the final C/T matrix it has to undergo a strict and systematic screening and selection process. Inevitably, in a company there are many more innovation project ideas compared either to resources or their individual chances of being solved. One of the techniques which is fairly widely used is to compare the technical probability of success as compared to the potential financial returns (Figure 5.4). Depending on the type of business, the techniques of measuring these two parameters vary. But as visually depicted in Figure 5.4, raising the level of well-calculated risks invariably tends to raise the levels of rewards. The method of selecting projects or even the decision not to undertake work on some others in order to create a business innovation programme is sometimes named as *Aggregate Project Planning* or APP. Broad elements of a typical APP are outlined in Figure 5.5. Thus a key set of business inputs provides the basis for APP and the final list of selected projects forms the basis to establish the milestones for monitoring the progress of the selected innovation projects.

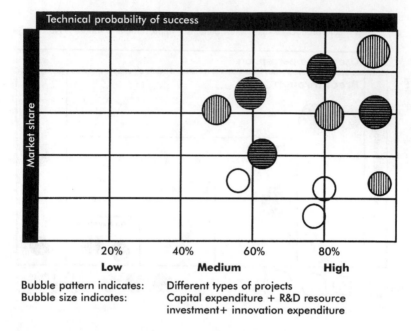

Bubble pattern indicates: Different types of projects
Bubble size indicates: Capital expenditure + R&D resource
investment+ innovation expenditure

Figure 5.4 Technical probability of success vs financial return

Figure 5.5 Aggregate project planning

Managing projects (Funnel)	Managing portfolios (APP)
Doing things right	*Doing the right things*
■ prepare detailed project brief (charter)	■ align technology with business strategy
■ establish detailed project plan	■ decide on the portfolio of projects
■ manage project in the funnel	■ place project in the funnel
■ lead activities towards delivery	■ set criteria for project progression

Figure 5.6 Key elements of innovation process management

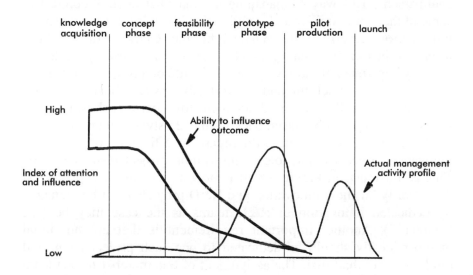

Figure 5.7 Timing and impact of management attention and influence[41]

Wheelright and Clark[41] have made two other major contributions which have significant influence on how innovation projects are managed. Figure 5.7 is a pictorial depiction of the critical role of top management in determining the successful handling of innovation projects. Throughout this book it is emphasised that in companies which adopt the philosophy of business-driven R&D, the strategic trigger is controlled and led by the heads of business and R&D jointly. Thus their responsibility, accountability and leadership practically influence all decisions regarding investments in programmes ranging from areas of fundamental research to choosing technology clusters and finally agreeing the APP of innovation projects for a particular business.

The ability of top management to influence the conduct of business relevant R&D and innovation is therefore maximum in companies which adopt these management philosophies. It is of course understood that such top management decisions do not take place in isolation, but as is explained in Chapter 7, are collectively supported by senior managers from R&D, marketing, as well as key operating company chairpersons. This way of managing is somewhat in stark contrast to some of the more familiar and traditional habits of senior management intervention described by Wheelright and Clark.[41] In the later instances, historically, management intervention invariably tended to be fairly unplanned, usually very late in the life of a project and was, as a consequence, unhelpful and unproductive. Many business disappointments as well as the traditional mistrust between business and R&D in industry can be traced back to this old style of management.

The second critical issue with regard to efficiency of managing innovation projects is the role of innovation project team members. This is illustrated in Figure 5.8. It is now a generally accepted view that priority business innovation and R&D projects must be managed by dedicated innovation or R&D teams as the case may be (see Chapter 7). Another important requirement is that an individual member ideally should be dedicated to one such project team, and rarely to more than two. The assignment of one member to one team is most certainly applicable to breakthrough projects while participation in not more than two teams is the general rule for all other projects. This rule therefore restricts the number of projects that can be activated at a point in time by any business group or in an R&D laboratory. However, in a fair majority of instances, it has been observed that these important guidelines regarding project teams are not strictly followed. As a consequence, invariably the progress of a project suffers and becomes a prime source of management disappointment and discontent. On the other hand, strict adherence to the rule enormously enhances the chances of success and raises both individual and team accountability.

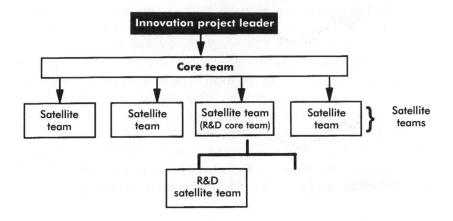

Criteria for satellite team definition:

i   Key functional area (formulation, processing, advertising)
ii   Key risk area (new component, claims support, credibility support)
iii Defined targets linked in with overall project milestones

Figure 5.8   Structure of innovation project management

Figures 5.9, 5.10 and 5.11 are pictorial representations of the different uses of the innovation funnel and the key activities in innovation management. In every case there are five elements which make up the funnel. Two of these elements lie just outside the funnel, one at the beginning or 'mouth' of the funnel while the other is outside the 'tail' just at the end of the funnel. The portion in front of the 'mouth' of the funnel is where one may visualise all the innovation proposals or ideas are assembled. At the other end emerge the successful goods or services for launch in the marketplace. Within the funnel itself there are three key activities which have been depicted. Each of these sections is divided into individual compartments each separated from the next by a go-no-go decision point. For example, as depicted in Figure 5.10, once the list of priority projects is decided upon, after screening a vast array of business opportunities, and based on the selection procedure described earlier, each of them is subjected to a detailed feasibility analysis to ascertain the chances of success. Only ideas which successfully meet the feasibility criteria are accepted and mandated as business projects. The conversion from a feasible idea into a fully-fledged project is probably the most important project team exercise. This is accomplished by a dedicated project team in a two-day workshop, described in Chapter 7. At the end of such a project workshop the project team produces what is called a draft project contract. This step is probably the most critical working methodology in the business-driven R&D process. The process, with minor variations, has been used for different types of projects ranging from proposals for basic scientific research, technology development, to business innovation projects. Whereas the application of this technique has been most widely made for innovation projects, its extension to all other R&D proposals has turned out to be equally rewarding.

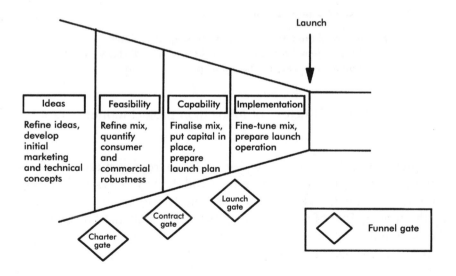

Figure 5.9   Activities in an innovation funnel

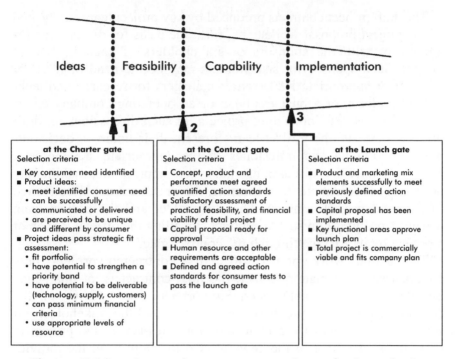

Figure 5.10   Innovation process – project selection criteria

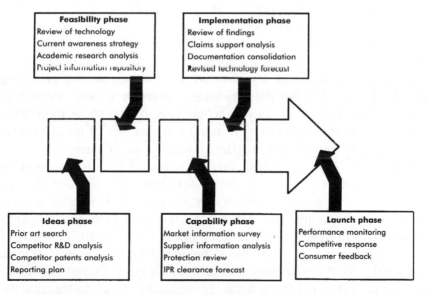

Figure 5.11   Good information practice in the funnel

The draft project contracts produced by key project teams at the end of the project proposal workshops, form the basis for discussions for agreement with the sponsors or stakeholders of each individual project. Such sponsors or stakeholders may be the head of R&D or some other appropriate R&D senior managers for research and technology projects, or a business head or an operating company chairperson for business innovation projects. In such discussions on draft project contracts, the project teams present their findings, decisions, work programme and milestones to the appropriate stakeholders. Following intensive discussions and, where appropriate, making any necessary modifications to a contract, the draft contract is converted to a formal project contract. The stakeholder and the project team leader then sign off on such a contract signalling the official launch of a project by its passage through the contract gate.

The actual work on an officially contracted project now commences. As a matter of fact, the final contract is, at this stage, installed visually as a Decision Support Document (DSD) on the desktop computers of project team members and the stakeholders. It serves as the principal means to monitor and manage the project in real time irrespective of the geographical location of all the individuals participating. A typical example of a contract DSD is shown in Figures 6.1, 6.2 and 6.3.

As the date of the successful completion of a project gets nearer, in the case of innovation projects, preparations for test launch and other associated activities are normally triggered. This particular step involves the more active involvement of the stakeholder. Major discussions are required to arrive at the final decisions justifying investments needed for the full-scale launch of a new product or service. The final phase is the actual launch of a new innovation following the implementation of actions arising out of the data from the prelaunch exercise and postlaunch monitoring (Figure 5.11).

Each of the steps described above is managed by a formal process with fairly detailed covenants drawn up along with appropriate fallback options. In the processes and steps described, it may become necessary, due to a number of mostly unanticipated reasons or events, to abort or terminate a project. The termination of a project at any of the three screening steps also has to be undertaken by the project team in formal project-termination sessions, which typically last between a half to one-and-a-half days. Such sessions are devoted to learning the lessons as to why a project which had been selected with all the due process had not met the criteria laid down for achieving success. Such lessons are well documented and fairly widely circulated within a business as a learning experience for other project teams. In instances where a contracted project or a prelaunch tested project has to be terminated, the stakeholder also takes part in the project termination workshop along with the project team. Such formal launch of projects as well as, on occasion, their termination, generates a very high level of transparency and accountability throughout the organisation.

One of the most valuable advantages in business-driven R&D organisations of the processes described in this section is the official recognition and sanction of all R&D and innovation activities. Under conditions of such disciplined management practices, any R&D or innovation activity outside the project mandate is considered to be without sanction and hence of no business relevance. Under such conditions, the spirit of pursuing some creative ideas or new research avenues particularly in R&D laboratories is provided for by allocating funds specifically meant to cater to such requirements. As in the case of innovation ideas, proposals from scientists to undertake work outside the project mandated mode, is subjected to a screening process by a committee of peers, prior to acceptance and sanction to undertake feasibility work. Some of the new ideas succeed and turn out to be relevant to some yet unanticipated future business need. Needless to state that, in business-driven R&D companies, such scrutiny and discipline helps to control the tendency of scientists to stray too far from areas of long-term business interests. In a few instances, when unreasonable conflicts arise between a scientist's pet projects and the views of the peer-screening group or the business's interests, the scientist may be persuaded and assisted to seek alternative avenues outside the business to give expression to such ideas.

6 Interactive Networks and Innovation

Introduction

The way technology is climbing to the top of the management agenda underscores the central theme of this book. The Internet is the most visible manifestation of how technology is radically changing traditional areas such as marketing and procurement. It is interesting to speculate as to what extent advances in information technology have influenced traditional ways of conducting business, or whether business managers have demanded these new IT products and the computer companies have responded to such demands. It really does not matter, because IT is permanently changing how business is managed. Downes and Mui, in their forthcoming book *Unleashing the Killer App*,[23] observe that traditionally strategy has come from the top of the company with technology being one of its constituents. But in more and more businesses technology is now the strategy. What is more, such strategy is built up from below, from customers and those in the company closest to them. The way to find out when technology changes from being an activity in the business to the business itself, is when it is no longer possible to tell where the business stops and the technology starts.

The way technology now pervades all businesses and influences performance has been described in Chapter 5. The creation of virtual IT networks, which bind the operations of a business across distances and time zones has radically transformed the way businesses now leverage competitive advantage. For the sake of contrast, it is worth briefly recalling how large businesses were managed until not so long ago, and how some are even today. In the old scenario, central command and control were the order of the day. This is now being replaced by internal knowledge networks which can be extended to create and manage external knowledge networks – networks which provide some unique advantages to modern businesses.

The only reason why knowledge networks are established by firms, is because they are the principal means to generate, capture and exploit new innovations from operations around the world. That none of this would have been possible, in the grand scale of today, without advances in the electronics industry and the explosive spread of IT is quite obvious. The success of business-driven R&D is an excellent example of this new paradigm, primarily driven by the power of IT.

Research development and innovation – a traditional perspective

As described in Chapter 5, big corporations and MNCs traditionally built and maintained large R&D laboratories in the geographic proximity of their corporate headquarters. Operating companies, in contrast, for obvious reasons are located close to their customers. In the case of multinational corporations (MNCs), their operating companies are located in widely dispersed geographical areas. In the early part of this century when telecommunication was relatively primitive and the usual mode of travel across the continents was mainly by sea, operating companies of MNCs were more or less left to their own means, to conduct the corporation's business and generate growth and profit, usually according to some annually agreed plans. That was also the period when long-term planning became fashionable. Long-term plans provided a sense of continuity when all other means of headquarter-operating company transactions seemed to be slow and discontinuous. This way of working can be described as 'empowerment by accident'. It was a time when technology also advanced at a comparatively leisurely pace and the life-cycles of products and processes were fairly long and stable. The investments in R&D in businesses in Europe and the USA grew rapidly, particularly after World War II. While building large and impressive corporate headquarters has a longer history, even larger business headquarters and large central R&D laboratories became fashionable after World War II. In order to fund the corporation's new investments, operating companies were called upon to contribute towards these costs. In order to impart a sense of accounting fairness, an operating company's annual sales and profits were used to calculate their contribution towards *head office* costs and *central R&D charges*. As their sales and profits grew, operating company heads found these two demands on their company profits rising annually. Usually the operating company chairperson would be less vocal in criticising the utility and costs of the corporate headquarters where, after all, the boss resided, but was fairly open while questioning the utility of central R&D to their own company's performance. The main reason for this attitude of operating companies, especially in far-off geographical locations, stemmed from the feeling that central R&D was a remote organisation of questionable utility to their own business. Such feelings were reinforced as central R&D also tended to drift closer to those operating companies which were in their geographical proximity and, in most cases, provided valuable support to such companies who were able to leverage their closeness to central R&D. Operating companies traditionally invested and ran technical development departments, usually in the proximity of their manufacturing units. Especially successful operating companies which were further away from the corporate heartland, tended to have strong and efficient development departments. Traditionally, these development departments helped operating companies in day-to-day trouble–shooting, cost-reduction programmes, product and process improvement and so on. The success of such organisational formations led operating company chairpersons and senior management to consider the value of their local development department as being significantly higher and more cost-effective than central R&D. Consequently, over a period of time, an unresolved divide gradually built up between the operating company and its development department on the one hand, and the central R&D on the other.

Another important reason for this attitude towards central R&D stems from an operating company's feeling that although there was a levy on the company's profits for central R&D costs, the company's ability to influence the central R&D programmes, in ways which would benefit a particular operating company, was usually minimal. Instead, the planning of the annual R&D programme was seen to be the preserve of the business heads sitting in the corporate headquarters. It was, of course, assumed that the corporate business chiefs finalised the annual R&D programmes and budgets after consulting all the relevant operating companies regarding their varied requirements. This procedure seemed good as a principle, but was found to be weak in practice in many firms. The weakness stems from the fact that, not infrequently, when such annual R&D programmes are set by corporate centre business heads, they turn out to be a compromise between available resources and business demands. Under such conditions of disconnected planning, R&D senior management have been known to fill any gap in programmes by supplementing with new R&D programmes, which they have presumed might be of potential benefit to a business. Under such conditions of inadequate central planning, the only occasions central R&D would be looked upon with favour by all operating companies were during times of unexpected crisis. For example, when one or more operating companies suddenly faced unanticipated competitive challenge in the marketplace, usually resources from central R&D would be rushed to assist the company – a service which was gladly received and well appreciated. Similarly, when product safety and liability issues arose or in matters concerning environment issues, operating companies were invariably dependent upon the expertise and direction of central R&D. In summary, communication, or rather the lack of it, acted as a significant barrier between central R&D and the marketplace especially in remote locations. In contrast, pharmaceutical, electronics and aviation industries exercised uncompromising central control on standards and specifications and used this as a means to bind world-wide operations together. In all such industries the role of central R&D has been historically more prominent and much sought after, but even in these industries operating company development departments are considered to be valuable local assets.

During the first half of this century, most business organisations were managed with the help of command-and-control structures. The effectiveness of central controls has always remained somewhat of a contentious issue. As has been mentioned earlier, these organisational structures were products of the state of communications technology and the slow pace of long-distance travel. After World War II, the quality of management by command and control improved sharply, helped by advances in telecommunications and the growth of commercial air travel. However, the growth of the modern electronics industry and the advances in information technology (IT) in the past quarter century have permanently changed how business enterprises are managed.

Simultaneously, the nature of traditional markets has changed and access to new markets has opened up gradually. The key event signalling the change in how a modern corporation is managed is the shift from the command-and-control hierarchies and structures to new and flatter organisational structures which facilitate managerial empowerment and accountability in order to enhance business as well as individual performance. The emergence of the concept of business-driven R&D is one important consequence of such changes.

The new communication revolution has probably had its biggest impact on the role and nature of at least two business functions, namely, that of the corporate headquarters and central R&D. I do not intend to discuss the changing character of corporate headquarters, on which there is now rich research literature as well as case studies, except in instances where it has an impact on the changes in industrial R&D organisations and their management.

Intracompany innovation networks

In Chapter 5 I have described how scientific research, technology development and innovation management have been transformed to their present state signalling the emergence of business-driven R&D. Throughout that chapter, repeated reference is made to the role of IT and desktop computers in knowledge management and the new ways of managing science, technology and innovation. Particularly with regard to innovation, its management by multidisciplinary teams, across distances and time zones, was made possible only by the advances in IT. The narrative that now follows attempts to explain how the traditional attitudes, ways of managing and competing both in central R&D as well as in operating companies in a business are permanently changing, driven by the computer and the information revolution. In Chapter 4, I made a brief reference to the question of the continued utility of large central corporate R&D laboratories *vis-à-vis* dispersed research facilities in operating locations. While there are conceptual and philosophical merits in this aggregation–disaggregation debate, in actual practice closing down or trimming down large central facilities and trying to relocate the scientists and other R&D resources nearer geographically dispersed and major operating companies turn out to be invariably expensive and unproductive. On the other hand, restructuring and modernising traditional corporate R&D laboratories, redefining their roles in a new environment of rapid communication, breaking down traditional walls built around nationalities and local loyalties, can and must be more speedily and effectively accomplished. Such transformations are somewhat akin to the modernisation of the structures and functions of old corporate headquarters. In addition to engendering this new culture, several European and American MNCs have started to invest in new R&D facilities in far-flung places such as China, India, Brazil and so on, in recognition of the differences in the newly emerging markets as well as the opportunities such differences represent.

One of the most valuable impacts of new corporate IT networks, has been to not only dismantle, in the first instance, the insulation and the isolation between corporate R&D centres, where more than one such centre exists, but even in fluidising communications and interactions between different constituents working within the same laboratory location. The tendency among scientists to be left alone to pursue their research work is widespread and well known. An important prerequisite in establishing inter- and intradisciplinarity, in order to tackle complex scientific problems, is the dismantling of barriers and isolation practised by individuals and even groups of research scientists. The process of facilitating the level and intensity of communication within and between central R&D laboratories leads to the creation of what has sometimes been described as a *borderless* culture.

The emergence of such modern borderless R&D facilities and mindsets has become possible only because of advances in IT and electronic transactions. It is therefore not very difficult to visualise that the same tools and techniques are being made use of to establish new connectivity between central R&D units and operating companies. But before describing how such transformations are taking place it is necessary to underscore that modern management practices and processes can be built on the foundations of traditional R&D set-ups in industry. In those instances where it is possible to homogenise and modernise traditional beliefs and work practices in R&D laboratories, it may not be necessary entirely to dismantle or disperse the existing resources and talents. However, it becomes inevitable that many of the traditional ways of project management, as well as some old scientific disciplines, invariably fall by the wayside either because they have outlived their utility or, in the case of individuals, casualties take place among those who are unable to adapt to the new ways of working.

Particularly in the case of innovation projects, described in Chapter 5, success entirely depends upon the establishment of effective intra-corporate IT networks. Innovation projects which are managed in this manner also help establish strong corporate bonds between central

R&D and operating companies in ways which were not possible to achieve in older configurations.

Above all, the fundamental driving force, both in the operating companies as well as in central R&D laboratories of most MNCs, is to improve performance in an environment of heightened competitive activity and unprecedented new market opportunities.

Innovation centres are new entities established in operating companies and they provide the physical means to create networks linking marketing, development, market research and the supply chain with each other, on the one hand, and with central R&D on the other. Such formations are entirely driven by the need to manage innovation projects efficiently. Such innovation projects become the sole means of linking the marketplace to central R&D via an operating company (see Chapter 5). What follows is a description of one example of how the creation of innovation centres (ICs) begins to bring central R&D and an operating company close together in order to accelerate business growth and profits.

Once again, as described in Chapter 5, a key to the success of innovation management is that most of the new ideas for innovation originate in the marketplace, primarily driven by consumer needs and demands. It is therefore natural to expect that all and potentially new innovative opportunities are likely to be first captured by individuals working in an operating company, in any particular market. Based on deep and intimate understanding of local markets and supported by data from market research and other sources, operating companies annually generate a list of innovation project proposals of potential importance for their growth and profitability. Such operating companies' ICs are meant to be the prime resources to convert some of these innovation ideas into projects and then into winning brands or services. Thus, an IC becomes the nodal point to exploit new business ideas and opportunities. The establishment of such ICs in operating companies also leads to some other favourable consequences. An IC provides a formal means to pool managerial and other resources from marketing, development, market research, advertising and, frequently, from supply chain, solely for the purpose of innovation management. The other changes in an operating company's organisation structure, as a result of establishing an IC, are not discussed here, but suffice it to state that establishing an IC invariably leads to refreshing transparency and sharper management accountability at all levels.

An operating company IC acquires a *solus* position in a company as a result of it being mandated by the chairperson and the board of the operating company, as the key driver for the business. Reorganising the already existing resources of the company into an IC format provides unusual sharpness and focus to the growth and profit goals of the company. The IC project proposals provide the basis of the annual planning round between an operating company and the appropriate business manager in the corporate headquarters. During the annual planning process, the selection of the innovation projects for approval acquires prominence. The head of R&D and appropriate senior scientists also participate in such deliberations, in order to ascertain the role of R&D personnel to be associated with individual innovation project teams, as well as to identify the technology clusters and science themes which may be relevant to the progress of such projects. Furthermore, innovation projects become the prime link between a market, an operating company and central R&D. In this way, innovation projects become a direct link and establish a natural working relationship between operating companies and central R&D in a manner which was not possible in the traditional ways of working described in the previous section.

The processes by which a final list of innovation ideas are selected by any business group, as candidates for the formal innovation management process, have been described in Chapter 5. Once an innovation idea is converted into a project for further exploration, the chairperson of the sponsoring operating company is designated and becomes the stakeholder of such an innovation project as well as the innovation programme owned by the company IC.

From the above description of an operating company IC, it must be evident that such multidisciplinary clusters, to be successfully managed, require dedicated teams as well as other resources. In most companies, an IC is created as a new facility where development, marketing and other managers can work on innovation projects in dedicated teams. Such teams can be assembled–disassembled–assembled entirely dependent on tasks and business requirements. In this way, an IC becomes a novel work concept, born out of existing company resources and reordered to achieve specific business objectives.

Most operating companies of a certain size are able to reorganise their existing resources and set up ICs quite speedily and adapt to this new way of working smoothly. The participation of central R&D personnel in IC project teams can be through secondment of one or more scientists from central R&D to the company for the duration of a project. More frequently, such participation can also be formally established via e-mail and IT networks between the IC and the appropriate scientist, or a group of scientists, in the R&D laboratory. All projects in the business-driven R&D mode, whether in fundamental science, technology or in innovation projects, are formalised in common e-formats as a decision support system (Figures 6.1, 6.2 and 6.3). As such, these e-formats can be listed on individual desktop computer screens accessible to designated team members, as well as appropriate stakeholders and the corporate business managers responsible. The DSS (Decision Support System) e-format serves both as a day-to-day interactive tool for a project leader and the team members of a project as well as for monitoring milestones and periodic review by the stakeholder. This turns out to be a powerful and common corporate language to manage science, technology and innovation across a corporation.

In the case of smaller operating companies, it may not always be practical to set up the fully fledged ICs described above. It is, however, entirely feasible for a number of operating companies to be interconnected via the corporate electronic network, which has been found to work very well in actual practice. By establishing such innovation networks all operating companies, whether they have a locally owned IC or not, are able to follow the progress of any innovation project of interest across the whole corporation. Innovation projects of interest to operating companies without ICs are also discussed and chosen in the annual planning round process, described earlier. There are a number of different ways that such innovation projects of interest to operating companies without ICs can be managed. One of the ways that this is done is, for example, for the smaller company to establish a country desk in another IC company and depute one or more of its managers to that IC country to become part of a particular innovation project team of interest. In this way of participation, seconded team members not only contribute to the progress of a particular innovation project, but also ensure that any specific requirements of the market he or she represents are given due consideration during the progress of the innovation process. In this scheme, a number of smaller operating companies can be effectively linked to a larger IC operating company. Such linkages happen more frequently in geographical clusters since adjacent markets and consumer habits tend to have a lot in common. The costs incurred in such participative innovation endeavours can be shared by the operating companies involved, according to well-laid-down corporate procedures. The second and more widely used method is for the chairpersons of companies without their own ICs to monitor the progress of all innovation projects of interest to the company by access to DSS e-format via the corporate IT network. Similarly, all operating companies with their own ICs can be linked to each other via the same corporate IT network. In brief, no operating company may find itself left out of the corporate innovation loop. In order to enable every part of the organisation to interact with another in the manner described, it is essential to use common IT languages and formats. In such extensive and intensive IT network formations, described above, the responsibility of avoiding being overwhelmed by information overload primarily rests with individual managers. Furthermore, in order to ensure corporate confidentiality and security, proprietary ring fences can be built into the e-formats. In this manner of working, not only do all parts of a corporation become closely linked, but in due course these links become enduring and invaluable virtual knowledge highways of the corporation.

At any one point in time, a company IC may be engaged on a number of different innovation projects. For example, the project leader for 'incremental' (see Chapter 5) innovation projects is usually a marketing manager. The majority of such projects involve the upgradation of an existing service, product or a brand. A few others may be 'derivative' (see Chapter 5) types of innovation project which are usually an extension of existing products, seeking to provide superior claims and marketing position relative to competition. An IC list may also include a few 'platform' (see Chapter 5) innovation projects. Platform projects usually represent a superior product concept or attribute relative to available products in the market. Derivative and platform innovation projects arise out of superior consumer information while seeking solutions from technological advances. These projects usually have one or more team members from central R&D physically working in the IC or plugged into the IC via the corporate IT network.

In this manner, innovation projects whose success has a significant impact on the operating company's bottom line, become a strong unifying force across a corporation. In the first instance, the IC enables marketing, development, supply chain, market research, advertising and so on to work together in formal teams, in a way which would not have been possible in traditional organisations with old professional attitudes and work habits. The role of corporate headquarters becomes more explicit in terms of ensuring resources and agreeing priorities. In addition to the usual annual plans for profits, cash flow, capital expenditure and so on innovation projects become important indices to measure performance and achieve competitive advantage. By its very nature, this process draws central R&D as an active participant in the planning process, unlike in earlier ways of working. Eventually, the cost of corporate headquarters and R&D begin to assume some logical relationship to operating company performance.

Generation of new innovative ideas, of course, does not follow the annual planning cycle of a corporation. The spread of e-communication, or the more common desktop computer, now enables the submission, screening and assessment of new innovation ideas from all company locations throughout the year. It has been observed that enthusiasm to contribute innovative ideas is enhanced among employees as soon as an operating company establishes an innovation centre. All employees become aware that innovation has moved up to the very top of the company agenda and individuals whose ideas become projects get duly rewarded and known throughout the corporation.

In this new environment, employees are encouraged constantly to seek out new innovation ideas to improve business performance. When a new innovation idea or proposal is submitted by an employee or a group of them, such proposals are required to be supported by some relevant data such as a consumer need, a new technology development or some competitive activity. The logic for a new innovation proposal, supported by data, thus becomes strong. To help in formalising the process for generating and submitting new innovation proposals, simple guidelines can be drawn up. The first screening of new innovation proposals is usually undertaken by a designated group in the IC, within an operating company. Those ideas which successfully pass this preliminary screening are added to the idea list for the innovation funnel (Chapter 5). Simultaneously, feedback is provided to the individual or groups responsible for the innovation proposal, along with reasons for acceptance or otherwise. The manner in which new ideas are screened for feasibility is described in Chapter 5 as well. If it so happens that a new innovation proposal is outstandingly attractive, it becomes the responsibility of the corporate centre and the operating company to assess the risks and rewards of replacing one of the ongoing innovation projects. This sort of intervention is an exception rather than a rule and is, in most cases, usually triggered by some unanticipated competitive threat or marketplace event.

Brief explanation of IT tools (Figures 6.1, 6.2 and 6.3)

The basic IT tools used in innovation project management have to be uniformly adopted by all operating company ICs. Absence of absolute uniformity or any attempt to deviate from a given set of corporate norms leads to utter confusion and breakdown of communication networks and the innovation process itself. As an illustration I will describe four basic e-format operations which may be used in the innovation process and to generate a common language across a corporation. These are:

Team working	(TW)
Decision support system	(DSS)
Innovation project portfolio database	(IPPD)
New ideas capture and screening	(NICAS)

A *team working* (TW) tool is exactly what it implies. Once an innovation project is approved by the mechanism described in Chapter 5, the team working tool becomes the sole means of work planning and execution beginning with Project Team training and Project Launch activity (Chapter 7). It is the team working tool, rather than either physical proximity or frequency of encounters, which holds a project team together. This tool ensures reporting on a predetermined e-format, and focuses on individual tasks and accountabilities, risk status, milestones and so on, while continuously updating appropriate marketplace events and activities.

A *decision support system* (DSS) is a tool which captures the real-time status of innovation projects for use by the project team, while also serving as a status report to a wider audience. Such an audience may include the operating company chairperson, appropriate business managers, cluster company chairpersons, corporate headquarters' business heads and appropriate individuals in central R&D. In the same way that TW facilitates transactions and exchange between team members, DSS is the principal tool for monitoring, communicating, and transacting information on a wider canvas.

The *innovation project portfolio database* (IPPD) is usually maintained for a dedicated group of products or services. The IPPD for each such group usually has two elements. One lists all innovation projects which have been approved in the annual planning cycle, and the others which are work in progress in the innovation funnel. Each such innovation project data screen includes information on key objective, location, team members and team leaders, lead country, cluster countries and key milestones. A second set enumerates new innovation projects which have been added to the ideas list for a particular product or service.

New ideas capture and screening (NICAS) is the IT tool for the capture and management of new ideas, described earlier in this chapter. Many organisations launch an in-company Innovation Ideas website to facilitate rapid screening via NICAS. NICAS is also used to publish results of new ideas accepted, either at the operating company IC or at the corporate centre as may be appropriate. Since the website is accessible to all employees, it generates a degree of healthy competition between operating companies and between individuals from the same operating company to generate new ideas and, even more importantly, to be recognised for producing the largest number of new ideas after the screening process at any point of time.

These four IT tools are illustrative of how a common language evolves via an innovation network. Thus, while ensuring a high degree of managerial discipline and accountability, IT is completely changing the attitudes and ways of working in virtually all modern corporations. Needless to state that if this new technology is not adopted speedily and effectively, the competitive disadvantages can become fatal for a company. We have not yet heard the last on the advantages of the interactions between IT and innovation management. There are virtually unlimited opportunities being created by continuous upgradation of new customer-friendly software. Thus innovation and its management can only be limited by an individual manager's ability to keep up with the growing knowledge explosion. Harmonisation at a corporate level is vital for the smooth and effective working of IT networks.

A postscript on networks

The virtual networks which interlink and facilitate team working and thus create new co-operative work cultures in complex organisations, are now claimed to be related to some interesting social behavioural patterns.[42] Two Cornwall university researchers have come up with a mathematical model which can turn any large network of such human interaction patterns into manageable small entities. The process of simplification is seen as the reason why more and more large organisations are able to adopt new productive structures with the help of e-networks. Certain researchers claim that the model 'may also facilitate a faster diffusion of innovation', while some other researchers go on to observe that 'the key is to link well-connected people from each level of the organisation'. The Internet and the availability of world-wide communication through e-mail is shrinking such networks even further and thus helping the change process. Thus the impact of social factors, mathematical modelling, market forces and modern IT not only facilitates but also helps explain why new ways of networking in the corporate world are permanently changing the way corporations perform and compete. As far as the concept of business-driven R&D is concerned, it would not have been possible before to deal with its complexity and derive advantages in the absence of e-commerce.

IT tools – Decision support systems

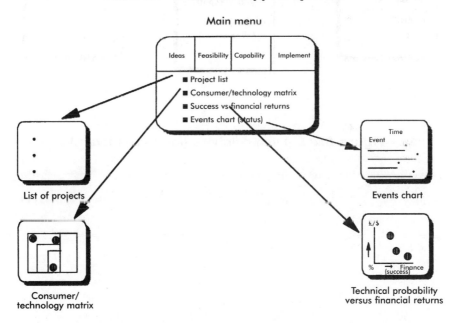

Figure 6.1   Portfolio database (examples of screen displays) for stakeholders

IT tools – Decision support system

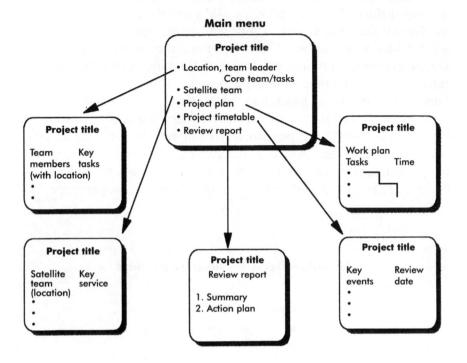

Figure 6.2   Team database (for project teams)

IT tools – Decision support systems

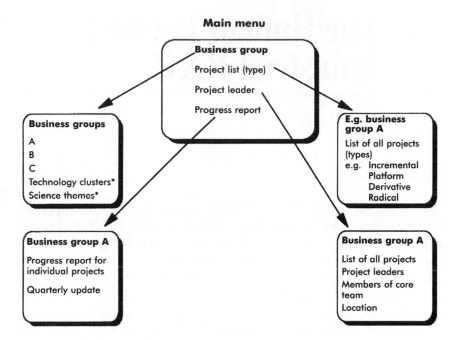

Main menu

Business group

Project list (type)

Project leader

Progress report

Business groups

A
B
C
Technology clusters*
Science themes*

E.g. business group A

List of all projects (types)
e.g. Incremental
      Platform
      Derivative
      Radical

Business group A

Progress report for individual projects

Quarterly update

Business group A

List of all projects
Project leaders
Members of core team
Location

* Similar screens for lists of projects, project leaders and teams, as well as quarterly progress report for senior R&D managers and head of R&D. Also accessible by business managers.

Figure 6.3   Master document
(for head of R&D, business head, operating company chairperson)

7

The Human Factor in Industrial R&D

Introduction

The human factor in industrial R&D is the single most important decisive element which determines output and effectiveness of scientists in industry, and yet one which has remained a grossly under-explored subject. While some of the great inventors during the first industrial revolution tended to be solitary figures, the issue of developing specialised manpower to undertake scientific research remained obscure until the present century. Formal human resource development policies for R&D specialists began to evolve in the German chemical industry during the years before World War II, traces of which can still be found in parts of the European pharmaceutical industry.

At the most basic level, the issue of the human factor concerns the formal training of successful academic scientists in order for them to comprehend the business processes and thus to understand those factors which enable a successful businessman to invest judiciously in science in order to derive competitive advantage.

Probably people who pioneered the modern concept of human-factor development in R&D are best epitomised in the USA by the Hewlett Packards, the Alfred Sloans and their more recent successors in Silicon Valley in California, Route 128 in Massachusetts, and several hundred technology venture capital companies which have mushroomed around most university campuses in the USA during the past quarter century. The myth that creative and fundamental scientists are not commercially predisposed has been put to rest quite comprehensively by the American academic and high technology entrepreneur community. British academics, in contrast, traditionally had an apparent lack of interest in wealth creation through knowledge.

Some experts attributed this difference in attitude, probably with some justification, to the British penchant for creative and original scientific work, while the Americans were considered to be better at commercial exploitation. There has, however, been a gradual change of attitudes in the UK and the rest of Europe, as witnessed by the more recent and impressive growth of technology parks in and around many very old and venerable UK universities, with the objective to imbibe and recreate the American experience. Similar experiments have been somewhat slower in the rest of Europe with exceptions in Germany and Switzerland. Now the European Union sees it as one of its main tasks, to catalyse collaborations among industry and academia with the express purpose of wealth creation and employment generation in order to raise Europe's competitive index in world trade. Japan probably has made the least effort to adopt the American model. In Japan, MITI's main aim has been to promote collaboration among Japanese industries, while Japanese academia has been left more or less on its own and venture capitalists have been slow to come of age. The experience of some Japanese companies to seek academic links in the West, which they could not do in Japan, by providing generous endowment to well-known American and European universities has been, at best, mixed and has not yet ignited the Japanese high-technology venture capital spirit.

The exploitation of science and technology to create wealth in the rest of the world, with the exception of Russia, China and India, has been rudimentary. In the former Soviet Union and China the most brilliant scientists were corralled into the defence R&D sector. They produced world-class defence technologies with which to wage the protracted cold war, rather than trying to improve the lot of the common man. China went a step further and almost destroyed its educational infrastructure during Mao's great cultural revolution. India, on the other hand, presents a somewhat mixed picture. Since Independence, India's policies were guided by the twin goals of self-reliance and import substitution. Both were successful, but at a price. Large numbers of the most brilliant Indian scientists and engineers emigrated abroad. Those who remained became experts in the application and exploitation of second-hand knowledge, which was the key success factor in the country's objectives for import substitution. India's economic development thus remained poor and stunted.

Industrial R&D remained more or less neglected in all three countries. With the breaking up of the Soviet Union and the economic liberalisation in China and India, the role of research in industry to gain competitive advantage has just begun to gain prominence.

As has been discussed in a previous chapter, the tendency to classify industries as high-technology, low-technology and no-technology is erroneous. The reality is that no successful local or world-class company will survive in the future without developing or applying some type of modern technology. Furthermore, over the years, the half-life of innovation has been dropping steadily. For example, the half-life of major innovations in the 1960s was of the order of twenty years. This has dropped to a currently estimated five years and is expected to drop even further. In other words, even with successful patented inventions and innovations, a corporation is not guaranteed long stretches of market dominance because of the high probability of being quickly overtaken by newer inventions and innovations. This rising rate of obsolescence is driven by an even greater rate of advances in science and technology, affecting virtually every sphere of business and commerce. It is therefore obvious why no industry can afford to ignore the advances in technology, relevant to its markets.

As a consequence of the changes in the nature and scope of scientific problems as well as their exploration, the method of undertaking research is also gradually changing. More and more, in place of individual inventors and scientists there are growing numbers of formal or informal groups or inter- and intradisciplinary scientific teams in universities and research institutions. The co-ordination or management of such research formations or teams is more or less left to individual institutions and depends on the abilities of those who may be the initiators or leaders. Some might argue that academic leaders possess a natural ability to manage, but this remains an unsubstantiated contention. Formal team working is probably more widely practised in industry, originally derived from the supply chain experiences dating back to World War II. But even in industry the practice of undertaking R&D in teams remained informal and obscure.

It is therefore somewhat surprising how limited an amount of research has been done on the subject of managing R&D, even in leading business schools, and in instances where the subject has been dealt with such investigations have tended to be too generic. Thus the exposure of young managers or even older managers in senior and very senior academic management programmes to the topic of R&D management remains minimal. The tendency of even successful managers and CEOs to 'leave it to the boffins' is still prevalent.

During the past few years, the creation of the position of Chief Technology Officer or the Chief Information Officer has been in many corporations an extension of, or in addition to, the position of the Chief of R&D. Science is surprisingly still considered to be complex and esoteric enough that it is best left to the specialists, with of course some vague checks and balances. This attitude among many businessmen is something which the scientists themselves have directly or inadvertently encouraged. Most scientists consider people in other professions as being quite different from themselves, if not in some ways inferior. Especially in industry, many scientists feel that they should remain at a bit of an arm's length from their colleagues in business, who are engaged in producing goods and services and making money. In most instances this attitude can be traced to the scientist's inability to grasp the complexities of business operations.

Scientists in industry, on the other hand, have a greater sense of kinship with their peers in academia. They try to sustain relationships formed during their younger days of scholarship and the bonhomie developed in the course of postgraduate research. Such divided loyalties are, of course, not terribly helpful. While most industries are proud to trace many of their successes to patented inventions from their R&D laboratories, nevertheless, management discussions on R&D funding remain an annual event which the scientific community in industry finds painful. In these annual rounds, the funding proposals usually get resolved notwithstanding a degree of hostility on the part of business managers. Such behaviour on the part of business managers tends to erode the self-esteem among scientists in the laboratories and they develop a defensive behaviour pattern. Scientists promise their business colleagues future results that would please the latter, but without the scientists themselves always being quite certain that what they promise can be delivered. Such events, in extreme instances, have been known to end up in complete breakdown of trust between business managers and R&D personnel, much to the disadvantage of the corporation.

The premise

The recruitment, development and training of potential managers into industry follow a set of systems and patterns which are fairly well established and are a part of universally acknowledged good personnel management practices. The Human Resources (HR) specialists are normally the custodians as well as users of such good practices in a firm. In most companies, the HR Department continuously updates and modernises methods to improve standards of recruitment and training by seeking out and following best-practice benchmarks from the external universe of peers and competitors. One glaring exception where the HR function has generally failed to develop and make use of such specialised skills is in many industrial R&D departments, especially in large R&D establishments. The major problems associated with the effective management of R&D in industry, as described in this book and also published elsewhere, can be traced to, and originate in the traditionally inadequate HR management in industrial R&D units.

If one considers the time and effort which goes into selecting and developing students for postgraduate education and training in universities, it is indeed very surprising that much of this screening and assessment rigour disappears once a scientist completes education and training and opts to work in industry. Peer scrutiny and other forms of assessment of scientific quality and worth, as practised in academia, are replaced by untested variants of normal business policies and methodologies. In most instances, such policies are not only inappropriate but also can be counterproductive for creating and nurturing a businessdriven R&D culture.

The gross inadequacy of traditional HR management as applied in R&D laboratories is a highly emotive and contentious subject and is likely to be staunchly contested by professional HR functionaries in most companies. On the other hand, strong evidence is emerging to suggest that when the HR function in the R&D laboratories is tailored to the specialised needs of a scientific community in industry, the result can be extremely productive and satisfying. My personal experience is that unless this critical issue of the human factor management in industrial R&D is addressed at the grassroots level and the need for a new paradigm shift acknowledged, many of the grand solutions formulated by management consultants, academics and business managers to raise effectiveness of R&D in industry will remain unfulfilled.

Tracing some root causes

Some of the root causes for the absence of appropriate HR focus in industrial research laboratories have their origin in the place of an

R&D department in a firm. Even in many prominent R&D-driven firms, with a few notable exceptions, the R&D division rarely stands shoulder to shoulder with marketing or finance and may be considered at best to be just about on a par with sourcing and manufacturing. In other words, R&D is not quite seen as being in the first division of the management's priority league, and is perceived as most unlikely to produce a future CEO or even possibly a main board director of the company. The possible exceptions are the historic practices in some German and Swiss industries. So, it is not surprising that high-potential professional HR managers are extremely reluctant to be assigned to a company's R&D division. The HR function itself is not well known to attract too many outstanding or talented professionals in the first instance. Therefore, it is somewhat unfair to expect an up-and-coming, high-potential personnel manager to feel excited on being assigned the unstructured HR challenges of an R&D department. There is always the fear that such an R&D assignment might reduce chances of further professional advancement. Career advances are seen to lie mainly in operating companies and other divisions of a business.

Senior R&D managers must, however, take a greater share of the blame for this state of affairs, because they themselves have never considered HR as the root cause for most of the transactional difficulties between them and their business colleagues. It is not unusual to find in many laboratories a head of HR who is usually a fading scientist of much seniority but who has outgrown his creative years. This tendency to find 'jobs for the boys' is not restricted to the HR function in industrial R&D laboratories, but extends to other functions such as administration, management of external funding, communication and so on. As a result, all these important managerial functions in R&D, and consequently the R&D division itself, suffer debilitating inefficiencies. Probably the only exception is in the area of financial management. In spite of this state of poor management, internal audit departments have failed to highlight such fundamental managerial weaknesses in R&D laboratories. As an aside, it may be worth mentioning that R&D heads tend to be far less considerate in providing 'jobs for the girls' where one or more maternity absences have ended many a brilliant scientific career!

So, if quality screens and standards for the recruitment and career development of scientists in R&D start being managed by HR heads who themselves may not have been very successful scientists, one can imagine the cumulative disadvantages which can and do build up. In one particular laboratory of a very large multinational company, because of shortage of funds, the HR head had a brainwave – why not recruit bright fresh graduates in place of PhDs. Graduates will cost less and can be better moulded into the company culture. Needless to say the consequences of this decision were disastrous for the laboratory's research programme. The laboratory director could have easily insisted that instead, with the funds available, the laboratory should recruit fewer but the usual high-quality PhDs without diluting any of the well-established standards. This, in turn, would have forced a reassessment of real resources and task-bearing ability, as well as future outputs from the laboratory. The laboratory head readily endorsed this 'brilliant' idea. There are several other such examples of gross mismanagement of the HR role in industrial research.

Another difficult problem faced by the HR function in industrial R&D units is the conflict of commitment on the part of newly recruited scientists into industry, between their former mentors and their new masters. The period spent by an individual undertaking doctoral or postdoctoral scientific research is normally much longer compared to the time required to achieve professional status in most other disciplines. The creature comforts and congenial environment of research laboratories in universities, far from being grand, nevertheless generate both intellectual and emotional bonding among contemporaries, and even between students and supervisors and sometimes with their family members as well. The glue that binds a research community together is the sheer joy and exhilaration of undertaking fundamental research, making discoveries and being exposed to different ways of thinking which tend to be unusual and original. Such a rich learning environment is unmatched in any other profession. And yet such powerful human motivational processes have not been systematically codified and scientists expect the non-scientists to acknowledge and accept, as quite natural, their different way of thinking and approach to the solutions of problems and tasks. Thus, in an industrial surrounding, the tendency of scientists to stick to their laboratories or to appear to be somewhat aloof and inarticulate, is misinterpreted as a sign of their lack of interest in the rest of the company. Industry, in many instances, has compounded this state of affairs by constructing grand laboratory buildings in sylvan surroundings, which are usually far removed from its core operations. This is done with all good intentions and under the mistaken notion that such ivory-tower-like surroundings are likely to enhance scientific creativity and productivity. Most national tax incentives for industrial R&D have also played a part in encouraging some of these traditions. At the other extreme, there are instances where industrial R&D centres have been set up contiguous with manufacturing operations. Not infrequently and over a period of time, many such R&D units are reduced to troubleshooting appendages to manufacturing or, at best, as incremental product and process development units.

Scientists who join industry look forward to continuing to publish their work in scientific journals, attending academic meetings and seminars and, in general, keeping in close contact with their academic peer groups. This is quite rightly encouraged, to an extent, in industry. A scientist in industry is aware that his or her future growth and advancements depend on how well he or she meets the needs of the business. Nevertheless he or she is also keen to maintain links with his or her academic peers, in order to keep up with advances in his or her discipline and thus to have his or her thinking continuously enriched in the company of his or her fellow scientists. If the balance between these two quite different sets of diverse forces is not purposefully managed and if it is left to individuals to manage the balance more or less as per their own inclinations, many scientists will inexorably get more and more drawn towards their old academic groups. The comfort of a somewhat relaxed accountability and open-endedness of time-frames in academia seems more appealing. In extreme instances, a whole industrial laboratory, in course of time, can acquire a university-like ambience and scientists feel more proud of their academic achievements and eminence and begin to resent closer questioning and scrutiny by business colleagues. In some other instances, following a spectacular discovery in its R&D laboratory, a firm gains unprecedented dominance in the marketplace and thus generates enormous profits and handsome rewards for shareholders. There have been such instances where the R&D unit then expects to be forever left undisturbed, as a reward. The unexpressed assumption is that only under such conditions, of absolute scientific freedom, can the firm be blessed with another spectacular discovery on some future day. At another extreme, R&D laboratories are willingly reduced to become short-term troubleshooters for the business. They can then no longer attract good scientists and acquire a reputation of not being an attractive place to work. There are numerous variations between these two extremes, the origins of many of which can be clearly traced to weak HR management in industrial R&D.

Some traditional methods of recruitment and training of scientists

Recruitment of scientists in industry is not radically different, in broad procedural terms, from recruitment of any other entry-level managers or trainees. Advertisements in science journals, websites, campus tours, contacts through peer networks, now the Internet and so on – each of these or in combination – provide the starting point in the search. Interviews, in groups or with individuals, are generally conducted by company recruitment teams which include, in addition to the HR manager, one or more specialist scientist. The scientist on the recruitment team is usually from among the brighter and younger lot in the laboratory with whom a bright potential recruit can relate. The team also usually includes at least one experienced R&D manager who can provide a broader corporate perspective. Once standards of quality are defined in terms of reputation of the academic departments, reputation of the supervisor, the individual's scientific achievements, evidence of the individual's originality and excellence, competence, interpersonal skill and so on, it is not difficult to bring in a steady number of recruits annually of consistently high quality to a company's R&D laboratories. It is only when compromises are made to make up numbers that problems begin to take root. Second, the tendency to restrict the geography of search for reasons as varied as nationality, language or cost, can severely restrict the pool to choose from. However, even if these difficulties are overcome and a laboratory establishes a record of consistently recruiting very high calibre scientists, problems may arise after a few years because of a poor fit between what a particular scientist was thought to be capable of offering and what a firm may have expected. Such mismatches take place in all parts of a business to varying degrees, but they get detected very early in main-line operations and are usually quickly put right either by providing additional training and support for the individual concerned, or by parting company. Such mismatches are usually extremely difficult to detect in R&D and it may take several years for a major mismatch to be detected.

Some important reasons for such a lack of a fit between a talented scientist and a laboratory can usually be traced to the training and development programme processes which are employed to induct and initiate scientist recruits into industrial R&D. During the first few weeks after joining, the HR department draws up a programme to familiarise a new recruit with the physical aspects of the laboratory and arrange meetings with the senior management, and finally induction to the department in which the new recruit will commence his or her initial research work. Usually within the first 3–6 months the new recruit may attend a reasonably well-programmed course lasting for a week or two, which gives the individual, for the first time, exposure to the company, its business activities, products, markets and so on. Frequently, also within the first 12–18 months of joining, a scientist may be seconded for a few weeks to one of the business subsidiaries to receive first-hand exposure of how the company 'works'. Back in the laboratory, the scientist would be well into exploring some scientific problem, assigned either individually or as a part of a team. Such initial induction programmes are found to be generally helpful by most new recruits to industrial research. However, compared to the other parts of the company the 'wastage' rate or the annual loss due to retirement, resignation or outplacement in R&D tends to be lower. While there are several reasons for this, a scientist who has spent several years in the university doing research and earning a professional status tends to stay longer in his first industrial job, compared to other professional managers. Second, the job market for scientists in industry is generally not as mobile as in some other professional areas. Third, the traditional performance measures used in R&D to judge a scientist's performance make it difficult for a scientist to assess his or her future prospects. Under such circumstances, individuals can remain in suspended animation for many years. Given this state of affairs and, in order to generate a reasonable number of entry-level vacancies, many new scientists who have worked between 3–5 years and show early promise, are seconded to operating companies, mostly in development or manufacturing departments, and occasionally to marketing. Invariably a fair number of such secondees to the business do exceptionally well and step on to the promotional ladder in different managerial functions. Those whose performance does not measure up to expectations return to the parent laboratory from where they were seconded, considered not as failures which they, as a matter of fact, are, but as scientists who now have 'industrial experience'. There are of course a few who benefit a great deal from such industrial experience. They return to pursue a richer and more productive scientific career as a consequence. Among those who progress in their career with the operating companies, many reach very senior positions and some of the more exceptional ones go on to become successful laboratory directors and business general managers. It may not be difficult to visualise that, over a period of time, a laboratory accumulates a large number of returning secondees. The general experience is that a majority of these individuals, who did not fit into business operations and hence had to return to the laboratory, end up as average or below-average R&D managers.

There are, of course, exceptions. A few turn out to be outstanding researchers and prefer a long-term career within research, without wishing to pursue a career in other parts of the business. Some among these few continue to be excellent and highly creative scientists and research managers and, occasionally, one or more of them even leave to return to academia to pursue their own research interests.

While there are several positive elements in the HR processes described above, it is apparent that there are no well-thought-out and well-organised plans and programmes to assist the advancement of the scientific and creative potential of the truly outstanding scientist. As has been described in the subsequent narrative, leaving a newly recruited scientist, after 3–5 years, to pursue his or her scientific interests alone or as a member of a loose-knit team to solve research problems, may have had some merit in the past but has, on the whole, been found to be totally unsatisfactory and unproductive in the prevailing business and competitive environment.

Designing a modern HR function for R&D

It may be apparent from the above narrative that whereas some of the more routine elements of HR management in R&D were traditionally carried out reasonably satisfactorily, the fundamental issues which translate into managing creativity, innovation and meeting business-driven goals remained unexplored. In order to design a modern and enabling HR function in industrial R&D, a corporation has to recognise formally the power of R&D to generate and exploit knowledge, with the help of technology and innovation, and thus provide competitive advantages to the company. After all, which other part of a business enterprise can genuinely claim that the bulk of its employees is made up of exceptionally talented and creative individuals who have been trained in the exploration and exploitation of knowledge?

In order to move away from the traditional practices of HR management to new ways of enabling and empowering research scientists and technologists, a number of well-planned and visible actions are necessary. The first and probably the most important step in any new HR initiative for an R&D laboratory, is to attract professionally qualified HR managers from other parts of the firm. Such HR managers must possess a very good track record, as a prerequisite, to head the HR function in an R&D unit. Not surprisingly, it has been found that exceptional HR managers, when brought in to head the HR function in a laboratory, tend to thrive in the creative environment of the R&D laboratories. They quickly get into the spirit of experimenting and exploring career and development alternatives, along with the laboratories' senior management. As an aside, it may be worth mentioning that the period spent in an R&D laboratory also provides unusual broadening of experience to professional HR managers, thus enriching their future potential and careers as well. But in order for a modern HR initiative to take off, the mandate for human resources development has to be clearly defined and owned by the head of the corporate R&D function. The R&D chief continuously refines the HR mandate in consultation with senior colleagues, both in research as well as with colleagues in the business who are the prime customers of R&D in the first instance. Incidentally, a corporate R&D chief who starts a career in industry as a research scientist and then goes on to become a very successful general manager in the business, readily earns the trust of his research colleagues as well as other fellow business managers. The background of an R&D head is an extremely important factor in providing effective leadership to usher in a business-driven culture.

Implementing a new design for HR management requires a professionally powerful and dedicated HR manager with a mandate which may run somewhat as follows:

We recruit some of the brightest minds from universities in order that they might seek a career in industrial R&D of our company. What are the key elements which need to be formally recognised, defined and nurtured among such scientists, in order to sustain the creative instincts of the research personnel, while they absorb, comprehend and solve problems which the business identifies as critical for its growth, competitive leadership and sustainability?

As soon as the above brief, or some other variation of the same, is agreed by the full senior management group in R&D, the professional HR manager is able to generate a list of issues with which to design the architecture of a new HR strategy for an R&D laboratory. The following is an illustrative list of such issues:

■ The rate of change in the world of science is so rapid that, unless special efforts are made to provide continuous learning and updating for scientists who join industry, individual creativity and productivity tend to erode rapidly.

■ As a result of the mushrooming growth of interdisciplinarity, it is no longer possible for any one company to afford to maintain either a steady state or a critical mass of a science base entirely on its own. Such circumstances necessitate the creation and management of partnerships and networks with academicians and university departments in selected areas of specialisation which are of interest to the company. It is important to recognise that such networks and partnerships are distinct and different from the traditional practice of funding external research projects and programmes by industry.

■ The speed of progress and complexity of modern scientific enquiry, and the progressive erosion of innovation half-life, make it imperative to undertake industrial R&D in formal and dedicated teams.

■ In addition to creating partnerships with scientists in universities, two-way flows of personnel between project teams in industry and academic departments are becoming common and highly productive. It is not unusual nowadays for well-known academics to be prepared to dedicate 10–30 per cent of their time as team members or team leaders of projects in a particular industry R&D unit. In order to sustain such high-quality working relationships, the industry not only has to be known for its investments in R&D of relevance to its business, but also for its ability to sustain a critical mass in appropriate areas of basic research.

■ Many R&D activities such as combinatorial library search, gene sequencing, chemical and biological safety testing, ecological monitoring and so on, can now be done by outside specialist agencies more efficiently and *cost*-effectively. The management of outsourcing is now recognised as a new specialism requiring specially tailored training.

■ The balance between large central R&D facilities and resources and ones which are dispersed and located close to operating companies is gradually shifting towards the latter. In order to maximise the productivity and synergy of such dispersed resources and structures, formal networks have to be established. The management of such networks and their effectiveness is entirely dependent on establishing dedicated project teams, their formal training, and providing facilities to link team members in dispersed locations, in real time, with the help of modern information technology tools.

■ The career planning of women scientists requires special attention. Thanks to advances in IT, and flexible working practices, it is now possible to plan careers for women scientists tailored to individual circumstances. Rigid HR policies have been historically responsible for the loss of large numbers of exceptional women scientists from industry.

■ Formal HR planning and design, specifically tailored for industrial R&D units, is sometimes blamed as being too prescriptive and consequently inimical to the creative culture of a research establishment. Original thinking and creativity is supposed to thrive under conditions described as 'academic freedom'. However, in many industries, following the introduction of formal and well-planned HR programmes, the general feedback from scientists is that creativity becomes highly productive under conditions of well-structured and transparent working methods. Scientists have also readily acknowledged that creativity without some work discipline tends to be chaotic.

Planning careers for scientists

The move from an academic research laboratory to an industrial R&D unit represents a change for a newly recruited scientist similar to what fresh university graduates encounter on joining a factory or a marketing department of a company. While induction, familiarisation and training generally help in crossing the initial cultural divide between university and industry, this process of transition usually suffers in an R&D department because of the historical lack of focus of HR management in laboratories. In the previous section we have described some of the steps needed to define clearly the HR issues and to modernise their management.

Once the work environment becomes transparent and modern HR policies and professional HR leaders are in place, an R&D unit acquires a businesslike work atmosphere, and the scientists can clearly see their role as they relate to the linkages between the laboratory and business groups, via well-defined business-driven research projects. Under such conditions, individual scientists are also able to comprehend clearly their role and accountability as part of such project teams. Even in the case of fundamental science research projects, individuals and teams seek the means to be absolutely clear on how their scientific projects may relate to the company's long-term business strategy, on the one hand, while ensuring that their research is at the leading edge of developments in that particular discipline of science, on the other.

Under such changed workplace conditions of accountability and transparency, it becomes possible to plan careers for R&D personnel, in ways which are identical to what is done for other professions such as in marketing, manufacturing, finance, and so on. In this way, the career planning process in R&D acquires a modern and formal structure. The career-planning process enables the head of the unit, the HR manager, the individual scientist whose performance is being reviewed and whose career plans are being made for the future, and the supervisor, where appropriate, to meet periodically and discuss performance and potential very objectively. Such a description of the appraisal and career-planning process will be readily recognised in all parts of a firm but, regrettably, has tended to be either absent or very poorly managed in R&D departments.

Following the introduction of formal career planning in industrial R&D units, some performance patterns are emerging which are unique to scientists and technologists. Here a word of caution may not be out of place. Formal and professionally managed career planning of scientists in industry is still in its early days and what is described below provides a reasonable but, as yet, transient state of play. The following description of the career-progression process assumes that the recruitment standards for judging the quality of scientific achievement (competencies and skills) of an entry-level scientist into industry, are precisely defined and adhered to. Following recruitment and after a two–three year period of working in project teams and with the help of annual performance appraisal records, a clear career pattern begins to emerge for each individual scientist. The following are some of the steps, as examples, by which a career pattern begins to take shape:

■ An individual has demonstrated, by performance and has also expressed a strong desire to continue to pursue a career in basic scientific research.

■ An individual has performed well in the scientific tasks assigned. The person also has quickly grasped the linkages with the business by working in innovation projects and demonstrated managerial potential while working as a member of a project team. Such a scientist may be encouraged to seek faster growth opportunities in operating companies, say, in technical or marketing management. Careers of such individuals are best advanced in close consultation with business groups, where either such a vacancy in an operating company is already available or may become available at a future date.

■ The next category is for individuals who have very early on in their career demonstrated a combination of high scientific calibre and very high managerial abilities. Such scientists are potential senior or very senior managers. The career paths of such individuals whether in the laboratory or as potential general managers in business have to be specially and carefully planned. Such talented people are immediately put into a special category and the company takes the necessary steps to ring fence such individuals so that they are not head-hunted by rivals nor allowed to be lost sight of in some other way.

■ In the final analysis, it is not unusual that even the most meticulously planned and executed recruitment process docs not guarantee that mistakes will not be made. Between 5–20 per cent of recruits, at the end of the first 2–3 years may be found to be performing inadequately compared to what was expected of them at the time of recruitment. In many instances, the individual concerned comes to an identical self-assessment even earlier on. The normal procedure is to part company with such individuals in as amicable and helpful a way as possible. Just because a well-qualified scientist recruit may not have been a good fit in a particular work surrounding does not necessarily mean that such an individual may not thrive in some other organisation or institution. In most such instances, it is worthwhile for the R&D management to provide assistance to such individuals in their efforts to seek opportunities outside the company.

The alternatives described above become a part of an annual appraisal process and invariably turn out to be of immense benefit both to the individual and to the company. In addition to performance appraisal feedback and discussing career plans, as briefly described above, the annual appraisal exercise, particularly for an R&D department has three other elements of individual concern. These three elements are worth briefly elaborating:

Continuous learning

Traditionally, scientists keep up with advances in their own and adjacent disciplines by reading journals, publishing scientific papers and participating in seminars and conferences. However, as a result of explosive growth in scientific advances, as well as of scientific publications, the traditional methods of keeping up to date with such advances are no longer sufficient for an individual. Therefore, processes have to be devised and plans agreed, tailored to individual needs, or even to meet the needs of a specific project team. Such deliberately designed plans enable the individuals or groups to seek ways and means to keep up with the advances in their area of specialism. This method of deliberately planning to keep up to date with advances in knowledge, and thus to reinforce skills and competencies, is generally called continuous learning. In earlier times, especially in industrial R&D, obsolescence of individual scientists occurred almost unnoticed. In an era of fairly stable employment it was not unusual for a laboratory to accumulate a number of mid-career scientists who were well past their creative phase. While certain individual scientists are undoubtedly able to be scientifically prolific and productive throughout their careers, there are a few who became very good at managing and nurturing up-and-coming younger scientists. Then there is a third group who fit into neither category, of either continuing to be creative and productive scientists or as good professional managers of science projects and teams. It is individuals from this third group who drift towards personnel management or general administration in R&D laboratories. Keeping one's competencies and knowledge up to date through continuous learning has become an urgent requirement for all three categories described above. While a few in the third category benefit by such opportunities, the majority who are unable, increasingly find themselves redundant in mid-career.

Working in teams

Working in the project mode managed by dedicated project teams is now becoming a fairly widespread practice in business enterprises. Probably in no other management process is it so critical or central to its success as it is in the management of business-driven R&D. Projects and teams have the advantage of traversing geographical locations as well as managerial and scientific discipline through inter- and trans-disciplinary formations. For example, projects devoted to tackling fundamental scientific problems are usually managed by teams whose members may be located in different laboratories of a company and possibly in some university departments. In contrast, technology projects tend to be typically operated by trans-disciplinary project teams dedicated to extract the results from scientific discoveries and transform them into usable entities, usually in a single location. Such science or technology project teams are in most instances supported by specialists in disciplines such as analytical sciences or environmental sciences and so on. There is a third kind of formation where teams are put in charge of business-driven innovation projects. Such innovation projects provide the direct linkages between R&D laboratories and operating companies. Typically, an innovation team may include scientists, technologists, development managers, marketing or brand managers, market research specialists and advertising experts and so on. It is quite usual for the innovation team leader to be physically in an operating company and linked to other team members in real time, via IT networks and project-specific software (Chapter 6). Usually the operating company is responsible for the ownership of such innovation projects. Such innovation projects thus provide a direct link between central research, an operating company and the marketplace.

The above account highlights the need for formal training of teams not only in interpersonal dynamics but also on subjects such as project management, risk assessment and accountability.

Training of teams

From this brief description it may be apparent that the success of business-driven industrial R&D is almost, if not entirely, dependent on how effectively projects are planned and teams constituted, how successfully team members work together and how well such teams are managed. Scientists are not usually trained to work in formal team formations in most academic set-ups. It is therefore extremely important to recognise this fact and build team training as a key component of the HR plans in R&D laboratories. It has also been established that generic training in team working and team management, while useful, falls far short of eventual utility, as compared to training in real-life work situations. From our experience, we have concluded that the best training can be planned and imparted using real projects to train formally constituted teams which are about to embark upon such real-life projects. Training with the help of real-life projects is facilitated by seeking the assistance of professional trainers. Professional trainers are encouraged to develop firm-specific facilitation programmes. This helps them to introduce project management tools and techniques as they may be made use of in each team's real-life projects. For the bulk of the training session, the trainers play the role of facilitators and moderators of team dynamics. In such training procedures, the trainers may assist a project team to disaggregate and reassemble a large project. This helps in understanding and interpreting the project brief, chalking out the broad pathways on how to work on the project along with fall-back options, undertaking risk analysis and gradually building up a working architecture model of the whole project. Such training also helps to define the role of each of the team members, their individual accountability, the project milestones and the project timetable. Real-life, business-driven R&D or innovation proposals are subjected to this iterative process during the course of training, using all the modern tools of operations research, decision-tree analysis and so on over a period of intense 2–3-day exercise. At the end, a project gets transformed into a project management plan. It is the normal practice for a project team to present such a project management plan to the business sponsor as the next step in the process. Following discussion and clarification, the team then seeks formal clearance from the sponsor to commence work on the project. During this final phase, the sponsor still has the opportunity to seek further clarifications, and propose such changes as may be deemed necessary from the business end, prior to signing off and thus signalling the formal commencement of work on a project.

The above description is another example of the crucial role of HR management in industrial R&D. The use of team training to launch a project formally is an extremely effective and highly visible means of officially recognising the legitimacy of an R&D or innovation programme as well as its sponsorship by a business manager. A similar training module is also used when a project reaches either satisfactory completion as planned, or a decision is taken for whatever reason to terminate a particular project. Formal 'project closing' sessions, once again, involve the participation of the whole team and are, again, assisted by a facilitator. Such a terminal exercise usually lasts between one and one-and-a-half days and involves a full and detailed analysis of progress made, or reasons for abandoning, and records the experience of individuals as well as the whole team. Such an exercise marks the formal closure of a project and disbandment and reassignment of thc team members to new tasks. It is likely that even before this formal event, individual team members may have already been assigned to new projects in anticipation or are now free to be so assigned. The build-up of the documentation from such project launches, completion and closures, undertaken formally, helps build up a powerful knowledge base in a company, for dissemination and wider use.

The project training methodology described above is effective for all projects whether these are business-innovation projects or business-relevant technology projects or even strategic fundamental scientific research projects. Individuals who have participated as members of such project teams – whether a scientist or a technologist or a marketing person or a finance manager or a supply chain expert – have, without exception, considered this way of working as being highly desirable and extremely appropriate to achieve speedy success. Quite unexpectedly, scientists of all ages and seniority have related back that not only is the project management and team approach exceptionally powerful even for fundamental research projects, but that the process of working in formal teams seems to release a burst of high-level energy among participants which greatly enriches the team work.

Some preliminary work undertaken to explore the reason for the uniformly high level of enthusiasm among team participants is indeed interesting. The process of working in project teams enables individual R&D employees to be able to relate the role of their research to the goals of the business in a transparent and unambiguous manner.

This, in turn, raises the sense of usefulness and self-esteem of the research scientists and breaks down the traditional barriers between R&D and rest of the business.

Another consequence of this way of working is that *all* work undertaken in a company's R&D laboratory, whether in the area of fundamental science or on business-innovation projects, has to be linked to a company's business plans and programmes. Any research work which is not managed in such a formal project-mode automatically loses legitimacy. The occasional fear expressed, that such strict formality may curb free-wheeling creativity, while legitimate, can be readily overcome by imaginative methods without compromising the discipline of managing in formal projects. For example, establishing an Invention Fund, which is open to all laboratory employees, ensures that there is a reasonable amount of extra money, besides the project funds, to undertake work on some truly original and out-of-the-box ideas. Senior management screening committees ensure screening of all such ideas, and formalising a process by which all new ideas which are submitted are either sponsored by the Investment Fund or the sender has to be told why his or her idea has not met the criterion for sponsoring.

A very important and related consequence of the introduction of a project management discipline in a company is that invariably the total number of officially sponsored, business-driven R&D projects tends to shrink dramatically. This drop in the total number of projects is due to a couple of important reasons. Experience has shown that a dedicated team member in any project team should ideally, and at any point of time, be committed to one, or at the most, two projects. There is evidence to suggest that if a core team member participates in three or more projects, the efficiency of the individual's contribution drops off quite dramatically and the individual's accountability tends to become fuzzy. The one-person-per-project rule has to be even more strictly adhered to in the case of members working on scientific mega projects or major technology clusters. On the other hand, in cases of team members who provide various scientific support services, it is quite usual for a person to be assigned, as a part-time member of satellite teams, to up to half-a-dozen projects at any one time, naturally depending upon the workload, the level of involvement and so on. Also typically, senior managers in marketing or operating company innovation centres are likely to be core members of two or more innovation projects at any one time. Adhering to the discipline of numbers in project management invariably reduces the total number of projects which can be activated at any point of time. Making the choice of priority projects invariably rests with research and business heads. It is the general experience that the number of project ideas with high profit and competitive potential are usually several times greater than the overall availability of company resources. The exercise to choose priorities forces major analysis and debate between the head of the business group and the head of research, along with other participants, such as an operating company chairperson, marketing managers, market research specialists, development technologists, scientists and so on. This collective process of discussion and debate on choice of priorities is underpinned by consumer data, competitive activity, current business performance, profit expectations, innovation intensity and other relevant factors. What eventually emerge as priorities are thus derived from a fairly intensive data-based debate involving the participation of key senior management. It is therefore clear that when projects are chosen through such an intensive analytical procedure, the management in formal project mode with project teams assumes very high visibility.

Similar intensive project reviews are periodically carried out for all R&D projects in basic sciences and technology clusters in order to ensure that relevance of the priority projects to current and future business needs continue to be valid.

The fourth consequence of working in the project mode is that major portions of the traditional hierarchical structures in R&D laboratories become less and less consequential. Here again, the role of laboratory HR management is crucial. The transition from time-based seniority and pyramidal command-and-control organisations, to fairly horizontal structures made up of team members, team leaders and project co-ordinators is extremely difficult and has to be nurtured with care to avoid chaos, especially during the transition. At least some senior R&D managers who have progressed along the promotion ladder and reached what are very senior but basically supervisory roles do feel threatened in an intensely goal- and task-orientated project team environment. This is because working in project teams eliminates the traditional supervisory roles. Senior managers have to acquire new skills to become either a part of the new team culture or become productive members of project teams. In addition, especially in less hierarchical and flatter structures, opportunities for personal advancement and rewards have to be planned in imaginative ways.

The role of the HR management in providing the infrastructure to launch and sustain a project- and business-driven culture in R&D laboratories, as described above, cannot be overstated.

Managing project network

The method of working in a formal project mode with the help of dedicated teams, members of which are more than likely in dispersed geographical locations and time zones, would not have been possible without the rapid advance in information technology (see Chapter 6). Since IT is one of the most important tools which enables real-time project management and team working and thus influences the effectiveness of individuals, a short reiteration on this subject in the HR section may not be entirely out of place.

For quite a while now, desktop computing and other methods of electronic data processing have had immense influence and impact on every facet of analytical chemistry, mathematics, physical sciences, experimental design, data processing, storage and retrieval, just to cite only a very few examples. This was rapidly followed by extending to time and cost accounting in the administration department of R&D laboratories. To train scientists and their supervisors in methods of time accounting as well as monitoring R&D funds, outside IT experts were usually brought in to supplement internal resources. Thus, although desktop computing spread rapidly and widely across the R&D laboratories, its role in improving the productivity of scientific research remained vague.

The move to the project mode of working and the increasing involvement with academic partners and the growing network of project participants in different geographical operating locations, posed the first real challenge to the use of IT in R&D management. Working in project teams means that the focal point is the project, each of the team members has well-defined tasks no matter where a member is located, and event milestones provide the means of monitoring and measuring the progress by all those concerned. It must be recorded to the credit of IT specialists that once the 'customer's' or user's needs are thus clearly articulated, they are not only able to get the appropriate software to service what has come to be known as the Project Management Decision Support System (DSS), but they are able to go a step further and provide the methodology which facilitates the project planning process which lies at the heart of project team training. In addition, they also developed new methodologies to analyse and monitor the sources and uses of human and financial resources. A common DSS methodology takes a long time to be adopted across a concern, but once the discipline is in place it amazingly facilitates real-time exchange of data and information of the work in progress among team members. Furthermore, it builds up a working relationship across geographical and time zones which would not have been possible without an IT software specifically tailored for the purpose.

Concluding remarks

More than in any other business management activity, the Human Factor occupies a pivotal place in industrial R&D units. Historically, the role of HR in R&D was exacerbated by the distance between a business and its R&D resources, in terms of location, language and attitude. A well-planned HR strategy and its effective management in industrial R&D units is the only way to link R&D with the rest of the business productively.

A second observation is that since the philosophy of business-driven R&D evolves from a mandate which has ownership both in research and in the operating business, it receives complete support and commitment at all levels of management. By its very nature of transparency and consultative dialogue, managing in the project mode removes ambiguity, apprehension and uncertainty among scientists and one witnesses an almost visible release of their productive energies.

A third element is that a formal process for career progression and performance assessment makes it abundantly clear that a career in research in industry no longer guarantees lifelong employment. Employment can only be ensured by continuous superior performance, continuous learning and the ability to work productively in inter- and intradisciplinary teams in appropriate areas of science, technology or innovation. Outplacement of scientists who do not fulfil the above criteria need not automatically signal redundancy. While outplacement of an individual scientist may be a consequence of a lack of fit in an organisation, the concerned scientist's talents might be more appropriate in some other institutions or even in an academic set-up. Such early outplacements eliminate progressive accumulation of scientists who are well past their creative or managerial peak but have to be accommodated, somehow.

Fourth, developing modern HR management methods and applying them consistently, generates a sense of confidence and self-esteem among the vast majority in an industrial R&D set-up. The dialogue with business becomes focused and task-orientated rather than merely being in terms of cost or acrimony about real or imagined failures of R&D. Business managers also respond very positively to a change into a new business-responsive culture in research. In such an environment, business leaders find it easier to discuss their business vision and ambitions with their research colleagues rather than being bombarded by high-sounding promises of what science could do for the business. Business-research discussions ultimately lead to the identification of business priorities which are converted into real life business-driven R&D projects. Research, in turn, is able to relate to the projects in terms of tasks, milestones and delivery targets. The process of working in project teams across time and geographical zones has become possible only because of modern IT and access to software appropriate for such team working.

Finally, a word of caution. The process described can be extremely rewarding provided the exercise is led and managed by highly committed and able Research Managers, supported by competent, professional HR managers. Business-driven R&D demands a cultural shift of major dimensions. To be deeply grafted, it requires the long-term and sustained commitment of the top management in a company. Frankly, given today's market conditions, a company has no other option. The old style of managing HR in research has ended up being discredited because it neither advanced the cause of science nor that of the business which invested in science. The fundamental role of HR management in operationalising business-driven R&D underscores the need to assign some of the most outstanding HR managers to the R&D laboratories in a company.

8 Tracking and Assessing Risks

Introduction

In Chapter 5, the basic elements of the business-driven R&D process have been described as being absolutely essential to raise the productivity for basic scientific research, technology development and innovation management. The role of networks and partnerships in facilitating the business-driven management process is the topic of Chapter 6. While how the crucial role of people and its impact on business-driven R&D continues to remain a most under-explored subject, is described in Chapter 7. There are very few well-designed HR programmes available specifically to train new research scientists recruited into industry, and introduce them to the nature of business and commerce. Even more glaring is the fact that, with few exceptions, the vast majority of CEOs and business heads have devoted very little effort to comprehending even the rudimentary aspects of how success in scientific research leads to wealth creation. This is in spite of the fact that in industry, investment in R&D has on the whole kept growing. Some of these attitudes in industry can be traced back to the disappointments of the 1960s, 70s and 80s. For example, the first nuclear explosion ending World War II was seen as the triumph of modern science in this century. But subsequent disappointments in the business of nuclear power generation are probably the most glaring example of underestimating scientific and technological risks inherent in what appear to be unusual opportunities, in recent times. Kennedy's 'man on the moon' project and its spectacular success generated high levels of the 'feel-good factor' in America, but its multiplier effect on civilian space research was not proportionate to the costs incurred by the Kennedy administration. Nevertheless the rewards from most modern scientific advances would not have become available without state funding of blue-sky research, an area where industry has very little to claim. The extremely high levels of uncertainties in blue-sky exploration necessitate taking very high risks, which only the state can bear. Thus, whether it is the discovery of the transistor or the silicon chip or fundamental advances in genetics or the development of modern IT, it would not have been possible without massive state sponsorship.

In this chapter I will discuss risk assessment in industry's investments in basic research as well as innovation, but not risks involved in state-sponsored blue-sky scientific explorations. It is however important to underscore that without state sponsorship of blue-sky scientific research much of the business growth in Western Europe and the USA would not have taken place. In a manner of speaking, the state's ability to take risks is infinitely greater than a firm's. Among advanced economies, Japan is somewhat of an exception to this phenomenon. Its application and adaptation of science to drive business growth has been attributed to Japan's different approach to knowledge management (see Chapter 3). At least some of its current woes may be attributed to this approach. In the former Soviet Union and China, state-sponsored blue-sky research was dedicated to their defence sectors and had very little or no impact in the civilian sector.

The state's ability to sponsor high-risk programmes to explore the unknown in nature can, however, be subjected to analysis and assessment of risks and uncertainties as are being increasingly used by industries. But close and systematic risk analysis, of massive state-funded scientific programmes, has traditionally been the exception. Large projects such as the 'man on the moon' or funds needed to build more and more powerful particle accelerators or even more and more sophisticated radio telescopes receive state support as an 'act of faith' as well as a tradition of unquestioned confidence in the scientific establishment to act responsibly. In this way of working, a culture of not being questioned too closely has historically permeated across state-sponsored R&D institutions, as well as universities around the world. This attitude of *laissez-faire* began to be questioned in the 1970s and 80s because of rising demands of big science on state funds and an understandable disappointment about what was seen as the failure of science to deliver as fully to society in times of crisis, such as that of the energy crisis and subsequently other events including ozone depletion and so on. Thus a new 'mantra' of social accountability is gaining momentum all over the world. A higher order of accountability has begun to permeate among state-sponsored research projects as well as across the whole academic community in every country.

The increasing questioning of the cost of R&D in general happily coincides with the rising dependence of industry on R&D and new innovations for growth and profits. As far as industry is concerned, one of the key factors for its rising dependence on science and technology is because the half-life of new innovations has been reducing rather dramatically since the 1960s and 70s (see Figure 8.1). To raise both the productivity and the intensity of innovations, virtually all world-class industries and MNCs are having to raise their investments in two key spheres. One is in R&D and the other in raising their skills and competencies in the area of consumer/customer understanding. Both involve high risks and uncertainties and both disciplines try to buffer some of the risks by formally linking with state-sponsored research institutions and universities. However, understanding and dealing with risks involved in a period marked by rising dependence on the success of R&D and sharpening the knowledge of market behaviour, has now acquired unprecedented urgency. As a consequence, the techniques of risk-profile definition and risk-assessment practices in most industries are having to be modernised and applied to areas ranging from fundamental scientific research, research in partnership with academia to innovation projects ranging from incremental to radical improvements of products or services as well as all those activities which lie in between. It is not the intention in this chapter to reiterate the well-documented and modern concepts of managing risks, rather it is to describe the application of some of these known methods in business-driven R&D management.

Managing risk in projects – basic research, technology development and innovation

In Chapter 5 I described how the funnel serves as a useful working tool in the management of business-driven R&D projects. It therefore simplifies matters if the same methodology can be applied to risk management as well.

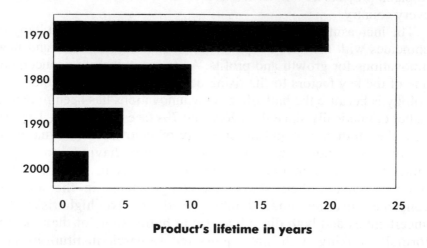

Figure 8.1 The reducing half-life of new innovations

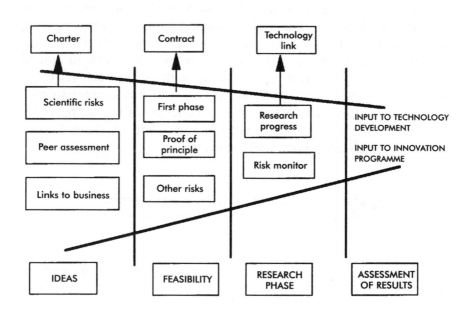

Figure 8.2 Assessing risks in fundamental scientific projects

The funnel in Figure 8.2 happens to be the same as described in Chapter 5. Each segment of the funnel, for example ideas, feasibility, capability and implementation, can be used to define a risk profile and documented as well. While the documents shown in Figure 8.2 relate to innovation projects, identical documents can be prepared for projects in basic research as well as for technology development projects. What follows is a brief description of elements of risk management in basic research and technology development projects and a reasonably detailed description in the case of innovation projects. Naturally both the methodology and the procedures will vary from industry to industry. Nevertheless the broad aspects described can still have wider relevance.

Basic research projects

We have already described in Chapters 5 and 6 how all industrial R&D units, in order to sustain their business relevance, must earmark a certain part of their R&D budget for investing in fundamental science projects. Such science projects dedicated to business–R&D programmes have to be related to the short-, medium- and long-term goals of a business. An important feature of basic research projects is that work on these is usually undertaken in collaboration with external academic and/or other institutional partners. The risk analysis of such projects begins with the construction of a proposed project risk profile involving all the participants.

Building a risk profile

Basically a risk profile helps to define the boundary conditions of either a large scientific theme, of interest to a company, or even a single specific project funded by a company. A comprehensive statement of the state of scientific advance, current and anticipated, in a particular area, and its exploitable or anticipated impact in a particular business sphere, provides most of the elements needed to build a risk framework. For example, while most businesses are expected to have a fairly robust understanding of how the Internet may provide it and its rivals with certain competitive opportunities, it may decide to invest in research programmes related to development of a new generation of chips or even faster and more novel processors and software in order to gain an early competitive lead. Similarly, key players in the pharmaceutical industry would already have built well-crafted risk profiles in their businesses, by assessing the impact of the human genome programme. In a similar context, it is worth noting that the public debate and controversy relating to biotechnology applications in agriculture and food processing can, at least partially, be traced to the incomplete nature of such risk profiles developed by the concerned industries.

Expert assessment of risk profiles

In the choice and formulation of basic research projects or large scientific themes or clusters by an industrial R&D laboratory, the tradition of peer evaluation and assessment plays a central role. The choice and selection of peer groups for project evaluation and risk assessment is made from among eminent academic specialists, who ideally have no direct interest or involvement in a particular industry proposal. The danger of breach of confidentiality of a company's strategic intent in any particular area of science by exposure to such peer assessment can be minimised or eliminated in a number of ways. For example, the peer group may be made up of individuals who are already associated with the company through other science projects. Other experts may also be included in the risk-assessment team so long as they are not connected with a competitor firm. The most important criterion is that the peer group must be made up of people of proven scientific competence, independence and prominence. In the final analysis, since basic science projects or themes tend to be both somewhat generic as well as pre-competitive in nature, the danger of loss of confidentiality is minimal in the course of peer evaluation. For example, a company in the business of developing hybrid seeds would be expected to have invested in plant genetic research. The assessment by a peer group of the quality of its genetic research programme and the scientists involved would therefore be considered a perfectly normal procedure.

Finally, the existence of a strong and modern intellectual property rights (IPR) regime in a company and entering into legal covenants, while inviting individuals to undertake peer assessment, ensure sufficient protection, even for such information which may get into the public domain.

Role of the project team in risk management

As described in Chapter 5, in a business-driven R&D culture even fundamental research projects are subjected to the disciplines of formal project management. Therefore, the assessment of a basic science project proposal in industry should begin with the project team workshop described in Chapter 7. The objective in this workshop is for a basic science project leader and the dedicated core project team members to reassess exhaustively all the assumptions made while formulating the project proposal, such as the scientific hypothesis, the objective, the experimental design, the research work plan, the risks and the fall-back options, as well as the milestones and measures. The core team of a basic science project is usually made up of industrial research scientists, along with some academic or other external participants. More often than not in such projects, the core team is supported by specialists from a number of important service functions such as analysis and safety, as well as experts dealing with regulatory and IPR issues. These experts, in addition to clarifying their own role in the project, play an important role in assessing risks to a particular basic science project. At the end of such a basic science project workshop, in addition to producing a clear work plan and programme, it is useful to make it mandatory to document the risk profile, the major components which make up the profile and the possible ways of dealing with each of them.

As already discussed, at the conclusion of a basic science project workshop, the team leader and members of his core team present their research project work plan, along with risk profile, to the stakeholder. The stakeholders for basic research projects are usually drawn from the ranks of very senior research managers responsible for a particular area of science in the company. For example, in a pharmaceutical company a new molecule discovery project plan for cardiovascular disease may be presented to the head of cardiovascular research, as the stakeholder.

Following discussion with the stakeholder, if a research project meets with approval in terms of business relevance, the project team is then required to produce a formal project *charter*. The inclusion of a project in a charter list signals the official sanction of a basic science project. Next follows the feasibility phase which enables the project team to commence work in order to gather data with which to provide proof of principle of the hypothesis on which the project is based.

Preliminary experimental success, which is more or less in conso-
nance with published results of other scientists working in adjacent
areas, then provides the preliminary confirmation and the basis to
draw up a *basic science research project contract*. A project draft
contract provides a second and probably the most important opportunity to a stakeholder to raise any further queries regarding the project
and, in extreme cases, due to a number of unanticipated but adverse
developments, a stakeholder may request the termination of a project
at this fairly early stage.

A *project contract* also provides the basis for annual funding allocation for basic science following discussion between the head of
R&D, heads of businesses and eventually the CEO of the company.
An important use of a project contract is a fairly early understanding
of how the results of a particular science project might benefit some
innovation plan and programme of a business unit. Because of the
high level of uncertainty inherent in basic scientific research, the
risks which are defined and built into a project contract are comparatively higher compared to other R&D activities such as technology
cluster development or innovation project management. It is therefore generally understood that a company accepts such higher risks in
projects whose success determines some of the long-term rewards.

Monitoring risk

Normally, most business–R&D programmes would include a few
large scientific themes of relevance to the business. Each such theme
may be made up of a few to several basic research projects depending
on the nature of a particular industry. In the project management
process described until now, each science theme is thus the end
product of a number of individual *project contracts of science projects*
related to the theme. Each contract and the progress of its milestones
are normally reviewed once a year between R&D and business
managers. An R&D manager, who may be the stakeholder of one or
more such contracts, may review progress and the status of various
risks in each contract two or even three times a year.

Usually such close monitoring of risks has been found to be of
enormous help. Such assessment may confirm progress as per plan or
lack of progress as a result of unanticipated developments. Further-

more, such close scrutiny of science programmes has often alerted team members to unanticipated but positive fall-outs.

Such methods of risk assessment and monitoring can be readily extended to externally funded projects as well.

Technology projects (Figure 8.3)

As described in Chapter 5, technology clusters provide the linkage to translate scientific research results into instruments with which to drive innovation projects. Looking at it another way, scientific research results may be visualised as software with which to operate the technology hardware required for the management of innovation. Each technology cluster is made up of at least one, but more usually several, technology projects. Usually one or more technology projects are deployed to make up the interface between basic research and an appropriate set of business-driven innovation projects. Therefore, the health of technology projects and clusters is of vital importance to R&D managers and their counterparts in the business units. To an R&D manager the quality and utility of a technology project or cluster is a reflection of the quality of basic scientific research output. To a business manager a technology project represents the fruits of investment in R&D with which to drive the business's innovation programme.

The risk assessment of any proposed technology project is therefore usually undertaken jointly by R&D managers and business heads, even if the R&D manager happens to be the formal stakeholder of a project.

Role of project team

The role of a technology project team in risk management is more or less identical to what was described for the science projects in the previous section. There are however a few important differences as well. Dedicated technology project teams are usually made up of members drawn from central R&D and a few from operating company innovation centres. In a few instances, external experts are co-opted into the team. Another important distinction is that in the case of technology projects which are built from the results of a firm's major science themes, *project feasibility* becomes the first stage in the funnel, omitting the idea stage as a consequence.

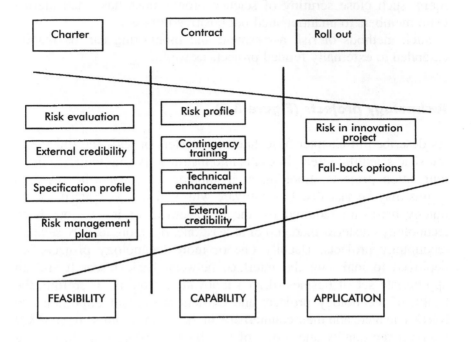

Figure 8.3   Assessing risks in technology projects

Other features

The other important feature of a technology cluster is its continuous renewal and upgradation. In other words, in a business-driven R&D organisation a set of technology clusters reflects its core R&D competence and hence must be kept at the leading edge in terms of quality, relevance and utility. Such a state of effectiveness can only be ensured by continuous upgradation and modernisation of each technology cluster in order for them to serve the business innovation programme effectively. The risk of erosion or loss of focus of a technology of importance to a business can be very high. The only way the quality of a technology project can be judged is by its utility to fulfil a business's innovation needs. And since successful innovations have to service constantly changing consumer/customer needs, a business's technology clusters ideally have to keep ahead of market needs.

Monitoring risks

In assessing the feasibility of a technology project, the main risks arise from two sources. One of these is the rate of output from the relevant scientific research programme which has to flow almost like feedstock into technology projects, and the second is the ability of any technology project to enable the use of the outputs of science by innovation project managers. In order to ensure the smooth and uninterrupted flow from science to technology to innovation, risk management of such projects acquires a critical importance. The purpose is to define clearly how the results emerging from scientific discoveries may enable a technology project to enrich a key technology cluster. It will become clear in the next section, when we discuss the management of risks in innovation projects, how standardisation, reliability and external credibility enhance the effectiveness of the risk management process.

Once a project team completes the feasibility exercise, the usual technology project contract is drawn up in consultation with the R&D and business stakeholders. Given their critical role in determining the success of the company's innovation programme, the technology projects and technology clusters need to be robustly risk-proofed by being subjected to both internal as well as external scrutiny by experts. It is important for a company to seek the services of reputable and independent external experts in order to reinforce areas such as the credibility of claims, environmental safety, public perception and so on.

The third element in technology risk management is the ability to assess the in-house strength of technology *vis-à-vis* key competitors. Such comparative scanning can be done by monitoring of patents and other published literature in a particular area of specified technology, along with the continuous analysis and assessment of competitive products or services in the marketplace. Torture tests of products or services are now a common feature in comparative assessment of technologies. Continuous in-house testing, under extreme conditions, as well as exhaustive tests in the marketplace, of products and services are now routine features in risk assessment of all new and even improved technologies.

Innovation projects

The method of managing innovation projects in a business-driven R&D environment is described in fair detail in Chapters 5 and 6. A successful innovation project is one that meets or exceeds the expectations of the marketplace. Achieving this goal depends on one's ability to understand market needs and develop products or services to fulfil such needs. Market need and performance are defined by a number of parameters of which the following is an illustrative list:

- the customers' interaction with and use of a product or service
- the product's or service's total performance *vis-à-vis* expectations
- competitors' response to the appearance of a new innovation
- the reaction of other influential external opinions to a new innovation
- the company's ability to supply and support a new product or service according to demand.

An innovation project team's ability objectively to assess and manage the risks associated with its project related to the above factors is vital to success. The degree and extent to which an innovation project is subjected to risk assessment depends on the nature of each project (for example, whether a project is incremental, derivative, platform or breakthrough – see Chapter 5). Risk management is not designed to be a bureaucratic hindrance to scientific advances, technology development or innovation management. Risk management is meant to better ensure the outcome of end results as they are planned. Technical and business risks clearly change with project types. By and large, breakthrough and platform innovation projects carry higher risks. However, it would be erroneous to consider that the risks involved in derivative and incremental innovation projects are trivial. For example, innovation projects which require major changes in sourcing can involve very high risks in terms of ensuring end-product or service quality.

In general, innovation projects are defined as 'high' risk under the following circumstances:

■ if they are classified as 'breakthrough' or 'platform'

■ if they involve high capital spending and major supply-chain alterations

■ if they have to conform to certain industry standards

■ if they involve significant changes in sourcing.

While the methods of risk assessment described in the previous sections with regard to scientific research projects and technology projects are extendable to innovation projects as well, nevertheless there are certain differences which are worth describing.

There are four generic steps in all effective risk management, and innovation projects are no exception:

■ Risk identification: identify all possible risks involved in an innovation project.

■ Risk evaluation and assessment: assess the importance of each individual risk, assess how risks combine and from that assign a priority listing of individual risks.

■ Risk reduction: minimise the risk and create fall-back options in case of worst-case scenarios.

■ Risk control: manage the risk plan as a part of the innovation management process and regularly reassess risks to ensure new risks are identified.

The risk management process described below is meant to form an integral part of the innovation management process. Detailed identification and assessment of risks and the creation of a project risk management plan thus become a core task at the *feasibility* phase of every project. Project leaders are required to ensure that a risk management plan is in place and is finally well documented at the contract gate. It is vital that the process is traceable and that risk decisions are documented in a way that allows them to be examined during progress reviews.

At this stage, it may be worthwhile to outline some key characteristics of the four generic elements listed above.

Risk identification

Risk identification is undertaken in two stages:

■ As a part of a project charter, the project team is required to draw up a broad list of the likely risks involved in their proposed project. A project risk potential checklist will vary from industry to industry and for different products or services. A typical checklist asks a series of questions focusing on the project's impact on a number of relevant areas. Usually from such a list, major likely risks, known as 'critical evaluation issues', can be identified. These are formally recorded for discussion with the stakeholder and to list the type of support that the project team may require to deal with the risks.

■ Once the project enters the feasibility state, in order to be able to draft a project contract, a full risk-profile definition is again carried out. This may be done as follows:

– by re-using the project risk potential checklist
– structured interviews with all members of the project team

Each team member may have a different perspective of any gaps between available and required know-how, skills and experience. These gaps then form the areas of potential risks for the project. This technique was developed by Halman and Keizer[43] for use in engineering and electronic industries, but can be readily adapted for a wide range of other products or services.

It is now also becoming a common practice to prepare checklists to link the knowledge base associated with particular technologies with the detailed information needed to use such technologies for a specific innovation project. Knowledge gaps represent a source of risk. Mistakes made in previous projects can obviously recur. A dossier of a firm-level history of risks, their management and mistakes, provides valuable reference material to project teams.

Using one or more of these methods, a full list of critical risk evaluation issues can be drawn up. Such a list must be a mandatory part of project documentation and it is the project team leader's responsibility to ensure compliance. The risk document is an extremely important source of information available to the project team and the stakeholder during discussions at the contract stage.

Evaluating and assessing risk

Once an exhaustive list of risks has been prepared by a project team, each risk is analysed, evaluated and prioritised before an appropriate action plan can be developed. To begin with, each critical evaluation issue can be elaborated in terms of what could go wrong. For example, a competitor response could take various forms: pricing, claim challenge, or an attack in an adjacent area. There are several tools which can be used in preparing a risk management action plan, for example:

■ risk diagnosis and management methodology

■ what if analysis

■ hazard analysis

■ decision tree analysis, and so on.

Risk diagnosis and management methodology
This is a useful method for understanding the significance of each individual risk and then assigning priority. The method is particularly useful when adapted to complex innovation projects which could involve a high number of potential risks which the project could encounter. The method involves formal group discussion among project team members and, as a consequence, generates strong team ownership of the risk management plan which emerges. Each risk is examined in terms of:

■ the likelihood of occurrence

■ the potential consequence to the project and the business of the risk occurring

■ the team's ability to influence and prevent the likelihood of occurrence.

The detailed methodology has been described by Halman and Keizer.[43] They have designed a generic questionnaire for use by individual project team members to rate each risk based on the above criteria. The integration of each team member's inputs follows detailed project team discussions resulting in the production of an innovation project risk profile.

What if analysis

The 'what if' analysis is a useful project team's brainstorming tool. The tool is used to examine risk areas and endeavours to predict the outcome of a failure in a project. It was originally developed to analyse manufacturing performance but can be used to predict impact of innovation risks across a whole supply chain.

Hazard analysis

Hazard analysis is one of the best known and most widely used tools in risk assessment. It also uses the brainstorming technique with a project team and its knowledge base. The method employs a set of predetermined key words which the project team members use to identify where and how faults may occur during the course of managing a project, according to a predetermined work plan. The process then helps to define the consequence of each risk and devises possible methods by which such risks may be avoided or overcome.

Decision-tree analysis

Decision-tree analysis is another widely used, structured and interactive, computer-based decision analysis tool. It can be used to evaluate the optimal outcome of key decisions in innovation projects. This is done by comparing the likely risks involved for any given weighted option, within a project, with the probability that the event will occur. It is a tool which can be conveniently made use of, alongside the other processes used, in the management of an innovation project.

Reducing risk

Risk reduction plans have to be prepared and documented for all identified risks. Such plans are again ideally prepared in joint consultation with project team members. There are structured methods of undertaking such exercise. For example, a project team would be required to establish

- why a risk is significant
- what can be done to reduce/eliminate it
- at what stage a risk is likely to have an impact on the project

- which team member is responsible for dealing with the risk
- how the team member proposes to deal with the risk
- and finally that the team members produce a work programme, time and cost plan for managing the risk.

Response to the above question enables the creation of a risk-tracking format for each of the identified risks in an innovation project. The sum total of the risk-tracking formats relevant for an innovation project enables the project team to prepare an overall project risk-tracking profile. Such a risk profile provides the basis to build appropriate fall-back and bypass options for the whole innovation project and all the risks involved in its management. Such detailed contingency planning, although time and resource intensive, is the only certain means to reduce the impact of risks while managing new innovation projects.

Controlling risks

All elements of a contingency risk assessment and management plan, described above, become one of the topics for review at every project review session. If any unanticipated risks emerge during the progress of an innovation project, these are subjected to the same rigorous exercise as described above under risk reduction. In addition, the original contingency plan is naturally modified to incorporate the consequence of the appearance of a hitherto unanticipated risk. Finally, a complete risk evaluation and audit review is undertaken at the launch gate. This is to ensure that all actions contemplated in the risk management plan have been dealt with adequately and their outcome recorded. Any unresolved risks then become a subject of key debate as to their consequence for the business, between the stakeholder and the project team members, concluding in a 'go, no-go' decision.

Weaving risk management into the innovation funnel (Figure 8.4)

In conclusion, it must be obvious from the above account that the manner of identifying and dealing with all possible risks which may be inherent in any new innovation project can be unambiguously built into the innovation management regime. Methods to assess and manage risks thus become an integral part of the innovation project management process. This strengthens and reinforces innovation management while rendering transparent risks and the way they are dealt with. The main steps in the process are shown in Figure 8.4:

■ at the charter gate, an initial document listing possible risks

■ at the contract gate, a document containing a

  – detailed list of critical risk issues
  – full project risk analysis
  – project risk management contingency plan.

■ at the launch gate, a document containing the

  – risk tracking records, with actions completed
  – status of the contingency plan and any outstanding issues
  – unresolved risks and consequences, if any.

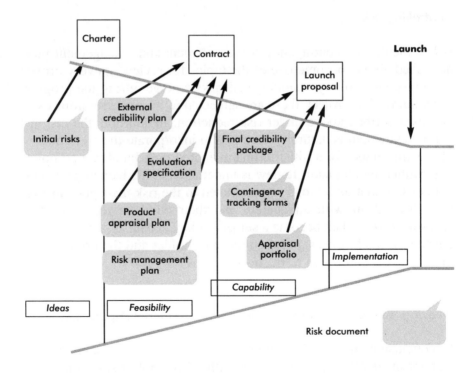

Figure 8.4 Managing risk – proposed inputs to key documents

9 Epilogue

I propose to conclude the text by briefly referring to some recent publications which underscore what this book on business-driven R&D is all about. That R&D has emerged in the 1990s to occupy an important place in the centre stage of business and commerce as the key driver for wealth creation is now beyond debate. R&D in industry will be at the core of all enterprises which will be the key players in the new millennium.

When product cycles were measured in years rather than months and competition was mostly confined to local geography, companies could take a fairly relaxed approach towards R&D spending, observes Paul Taylor in an article entitled 'For Leading IT Companies it is Research or Die'.[39] But times have changed. As Alan Wood, chief executive of Siemens, UK, was quoted in this article:[39]

> Micro electronics and software are determining the speed of innovation more than ever before. Product life cycles have become shorter and shorter, in some of our businesses, they have been reduced to *half a year*. More than 70% of products and systems Siemens currently sell world-wide are less than five years old.

What this means, in turn, is that at least 70 per cent of what the company sells at present will have to be replaced, refreshed or invented, in the next five years, if it has to remain competitive. He adds:

> A key to maintaining and improving our competitiveness will be *successfully managed innovation programmes*.

At Siemens, Wood[39] is quoted as saying, the *management of innovation* has two basic dimensions:

> corporate *innovation teams* at the heart of the organisation focusing on our core business areas. And a global *innovation network* aimed at maximising the talent, experience and expertise available in our operations around the world.

> Whether it is a centre for internet solutions in the US or a centre for advanced software development in India, the aim is to make the most of our intellectual capital.

Today, for most companies, maintaining or increasing R&D expenditure while *improving the efficiency of the process* is now a vital ingredient if a competitive edge is to be maintained. As a result, *R&D is a key indicator for the health and vitality of an organisation* – a fact reflected in the world-wide surge of investment in industrial research in 1997 led by US-based companies. According to the UK Department of Trade and Industry (DTI) Annual International R&D scoreboard, the world's top 300 companies spent £131 billion (US$216 billion) on R&D in 1997, 12.8 per cent more than 1996, while 133 US companies on the scoreboard raised total spending by 17.7 per cent to £59 billion (US$97 billion). Both increases were the largest recorded since the DTI began compiling the scoreboard in 1991. Commenting on the DTI scoreboard, John Battle,[39] the UK science minister, is quoted as follows:

> A key factor is investment in R&D, literally building for the future. Increasingly technology delivers new products and services. No company can expect profit growth tomorrow without serious investment today.

> the amount of R&D expenditure can only be a partial indicator; what really matters is the effectiveness of the investment which depends on integrating R&D with business, marketing and customer strategy and on the *quality of innovation management*.

Another important feature, Paul Taylor observes, is the increasing linkages of companies with academic institutions. US IT multinationals are leading in the creation of global research networks embracing development centres in India and Europe as well as California's Silicon Valley. Maintaining high levels of R&D spending is clearly easier when a business is growing, but there is increasing evidence that it is also a vital constituent of any turnaround strategy. Lou Gerstner has demonstrated this in his turnaround management of IBM. 'Well managed R&D is the solution rather than the problem', according to Paul Horn,[39] Head of IBM's US$5 billion-a-year research programme.

> *The commitment to R&D comes right from the top.* The technology engine will keep chugging along and if we do not do it, someone else will

according to Mr Horn,[39] who has put in place a highly sophisticated system for managing IBM's investment in R&D and ensuring it *delivers real value*. One aspect that is critical for success is the flow of new technology into the marketplace, he says in Paul Taylor's article.[39] In part, this has been achieved by reorganising the funding of R&D and ensuring that *it is closely tied to business objectives*.

In the same article, Carol Galley, co-head of Merrill Lynch Mercury Asset Management in the UK, made the following observation:

> Our key message is that companies should ensure that their *investment in R&D creates value*. In other words, the expected returns from the investments should be greater than the cost of capital appropriate for the company and its projects. To achieve this, the investment must be coherent with the overall strategy of the firm and be efficiently managed. And in our view, the level of achievement must be measured by the amount of shareholder value created, and *not the amount of money spent*.

Carol Galley cites Ericsson, Intel and CISCO as shining examples of how this is achieved in business practice.

Indeed, there is a *growing recognition among investors of the link between R&D investment and long-term growth*. And this, in turn, has been reflected in the share price performance of those companies that have *mastered the art of extracting value from R&D* spending.

Paul Taylor's observations are echoed by Dan Vergano,[44] quoting from a US National Science Foundation (NSF) report. It has long been argued the world over, that *advances in basic research lead to innovations* that increase the common good. Vergano goes on to state that in July 1998 an NSF Science and Engineering Indicators report described how *publicly funded research* is increasingly creating economically important inventions. An NSF-sponsored study of 100,000 US patents found that 73 per cent cited work emanating from academic, government or other publicly funded institutions, as the basis for their innovations. The NSF reported that the number of US patents based on public research has nearly tripled since 1988. Furthermore, in the words of the report:

> public science cited in these references was at the basic end of the research spectrum.

Some of the responsibility for the explosive growth lies fairly and squarely at the door of the information age, which has enabled extensive and rapid electronic searches of research articles. But there is more to the trend. 'We're seeing indications of whole science and technology infrastructure changing', says Jennifer Bond of NSF, one of the authors of the report. Partnerships of every sort – between industry, academia and government labs, on an international scale – are becoming the norm. In today's economy, science has become too big an enterprise for any one company to master all the facts needed for modern production. And with tight research budgets in most companies, academia are an ideal low-cost source of collaborators. Corporations also value the perceived independence of public institutions to validate their research. (Peer scrutiny and risk assessment!) In Bond's view, there has also been a shift towards *academics being interested in problems of industry*. Nations like the USA and Britain, she suggests, which have long histories of scientific collaboration with industry, are more competitive than countries such as Germany, where the rift between the two is more pronounced.

CHI Research, the New Jersey consulting firm that conducted the patent search for NSF, has also stated in the report referred to above that:

> companies that give the highest returns on the US stock market are those that cite public science most often in their patent applications Across chemical, electronic, biomedical and other industries, a statistically significant link between long term stock performance and use of science citation emerges.

If confirmed, it will prove definitively that basic science is crucial to economic advancement.

All the above observations are even more strongly reinforced by a recent review in *Business Week*, entitled 'The 21st Century Economy'.[45] While primarily describing events in the USA to bolster its core theme, the conclusions of the review have broader validity in the global context. The review states:

> we have never had a period in which innovation has so permeated our lives as in the 1990s. There is going to be a fundamental change in the global economy unlike anything since cavemen began bartering.

Periods of major innovations have brought profound increases in living standards. The last one started with railroads in the 1890s and lasted through the advent of television and jet travel in the 1950s and 60s. In the long run, the success of the 21st-century economy will depend on whether technological progress will continue to drive growth, as it has so far in this decade. That would be a big change from the 1970s and 80s. In those decades of economic stagnation, technology contributed almost nothing to growth according to published statistics. The computer revolution had yet to take off and earlier innovations such as jet travel were no longer new. But in the 1990s, the innovations have been coming back thick and fast. In part, the sudden re-emergence of technological progress is the culmination of years of research in disparate fields that are finally reaching critical mass. The Internet, which only became a commercial proposition in the mid-1990s, is the direct descendent of the ARPAnet, which was funded by the US Defense Department in the 1960s. The first gene-splicing experiment was done in 1973 but biotechnology is just starting to explode. Moreover, different parts of the innovation waves are starting to feed and reinforce one another, as fast computers greatly accelerate the ability of scientists to unravel and manipulate genes. Conversely, biological techniques now seem the best foundations for developing tomorrow's new generation of computers. The innovation wave is also being given more force by the globalisation of the economy. Bright ideas developed in Israel or India quickly find world markets.

Today's innovations have a better chance of succeeding because they are being developed by private industry in response to the profit motive, which automatically gives an incentive to seek out technologies that are economically viable. Nuclear power and the space programme, by contrast, were creatures of government and of heavily regulated industries, which had no such incentives. At the turn of the century, innovations transformed the economy as industry exploited scientific research and modern management as never before. Entrepreneurs built their companies into behemoths, thanks to the new techniques of mass production, the spread of electric power and the rise of the internal combustion engine. The same thing seems to be happening today. In economies driven by innovation, it is clear that restructuring, re-engineering and downsizing – choose any buzzword – will be a permanent part of management tool kits in the 21st century. Employees will have to keep learning new skills with each new upheaval. The only encashable skill will be learning new skills, and change the only constant.

The same article goes on to state that trans-disciplinarity will be the key to the high-tech landscape which is on the brink of change. For example, the development pipelines in many high-tech companies already showcase a whole new breed of miniaturised marvels with capabilities well beyond today's chips. Over the next half a decade these so-called 'microelectromechanical systems" (MEMS) – which combine sensors, motors and digital smarts in a single sliver of silicon – are likely to supplement more expensive components in computer hardware, automobile engines, factory assembly lines and dozens of other processes and products. The software for such devices is already in the process of being devised.

Going somewhat further out – probably 15–20 years – high-tech visionaries foresee a transition that is far more radical and disruptive. Its quintessence won't be smaller, cheaper, faster electronics only; what the transition scientists speak of involves nothing less than the highjacking of nature's own creative machinery. In medicine, this spells the ability to repair or replace the body's failing organs. In manufacturing, it means coercing molecules to assemble into useful devices – the same way crystals and living creatures assemble themselves. In computing, disk storage capacity could be increased a hundredfold by an MEMS-based instrument called an atomic force microscope. Such 'probe' microscopes, invented at IBM and Stanford University, produce images of atoms. The coming wave of minimalisation and molecular electronics – sometimes called nanotechnology – is taking place at the trans-disciplinary intersection of chemistry, physics, biology and electrical engineering. And if it crests, as many scientists predict, it will bring a wholesale industrial transformation, more dramatic than the late 20th-century flowering of microelectronics. Nanotechnology, at the turn of the century, will be a big surprise to economists who believe that industry has already reaped all the easy benefits of the Information Revolution. The revolution has barely begun.

J Craig Ventner, President of the Institute of Genomic Research and pioneering gene scientist, is quoted as follows: 'we are now starting the century of biology'.[45] The discovery of thousands of human genes and biochemical pathways is transforming the pharmaceutical industry (see below). As a consequence, companies have gone from having so few targets (for drugs) which were guarded like Fort Knox, to being awash in targets.

Signs are strong that Silicon Valley will continue to churn out new ideas and new companies for some time. The valley still possesses the combination of ingredients that nurtured Intel, Apple Computers and CISCO systems. The key is the sheer density of more than 7000 tech companies crammed into a 50-mile corridor. That gives start-up access to a deep talent pool of smart, experienced engineers, programmers and managers, as well as the infrastructure – from legal to technical to marketing – that can turn an entrepreneur's idea into a company overnight. Add to that the unmatched availability of venture capital and funding from larger corporations, and a climate that rewards risk taking and tolerates failures, and that is a recipe for a technological hothouse.

In the services, financial engineers don't wear white lab coats. They don't experiment with rats or perform gas chromatography. Their raw material – money – is not as jazzy as what biologists and physicists investigate. But the innovations they produce will contribute just as much to economic growth. Financial services will be almost indistinguishable from any other software business with continuous innovation and pre-emptive cannibalisation.

Outsourcing, a practice that has been around for decades, does not begin to define what is happening to manufacturing and the supply chain. In place of traditional contracting relationships between client and supplier, new partnerships are emerging as a sort of extended enterprise – a set of partnerships between product developers and specialists in components, distribution, retailing and manufacturing. The resulting organisation can be so tight as to behave like a single, close-knit company – only better. Its strategies can slash time and costs out of the supply chain, the process between the invention of a new product and the time it reaches the consumer. The effect on innovation can be huge. Outsourcing manufacturing and other non-core functions allows industrial titans to focus on new investment where it gets the most returns: research and marketing. Because the strategy reduces the need for capital and in-house operations expertise, moreover, start-ups face far lower barriers in bringing new technologies to market. Thus in many industries vertical integration is giving way to virtual integration, the article observes.

As virtual integration evolves, futurists envision a time when product developers, manufacturers and distributors will be so tightly linked through data networks that inventories will all but disappear. Companies will make goods based on daily needs of retailers. Even automobiles will be assembled to customers' specifications within days, just as Dell Computers Corporation and CISCO systems do now with computers and networking equipment. A sunset industry no longer, manufacturing will help drive innovation.

Describing a related issue, the article comments on the evidence that an R&D dollar spent by industry in academics has a much bigger pay off than other research done in government-run labs. Yet, left to their own devices, corporations will naturally focus on R&D that translates directly into profitable products. The more fundamental work of scientific discovery – the kind of research that has tremendous benefits for society as a whole – is uneconomical for individual companies with a few rare exceptions. That suggests government has an important role in funding long-term basic research. The projects thus funded 10–15 years ago produced a large portion of the stream of ideas that created the current generation of technology.

New rules of competition demand organisations built on change, not stability; organised around networks, not rigid hierarchy; based on interdependencies and trans-disciplinarity of partners, not self-sufficiency; and constructed on technological advantage, not old-fashioned brick and mortar. Networks become the glue for the internal working of the company. The customer is the strategy. There is nothing more arrogant than telling the customer, 'Here is what you need to know.'

There has thus begun to emerge a grand wave in the fortunes of humankind with which to generate greater prosperity and a better life-style, away from sweating the body to sweating the mind.

In an *Economist* survey of the pharmaceutical industry, the emergence of a 21st-century industry, entirely driven by R&D, is probably the most visible manifestation of the 1990s' phenomenon.[46] Many of the statements in this article reinforce the concept of business-driven R&D. The manufacture of drugs is one of the world's largest and most profitable manufacturing industries. Until surprisingly recently, however, the miracle of profitability and the health of this industry remained relatively obscure. This was partly because the scientists did not know how drugs work in the human body to make the process of discovery truly scientific, and partly because in what was generally a seller's market, there was no strong financial incentive to sharpen that process up. But both these are changing. Modern biological discoveries, particularly in the area of genetics, provide vastly more information on how drugs operate and how new ones may be designed. This will radically change availability and cost to customers. New technologies such as combinatorial chemistry, high throughput screening, and laboratories-on-a-chip offer better ways to turn knowledge from genetics into molecules for testing. The old ways of making promising molecules and filling 'pipelines' have become leaky and grossly expensive affairs. It has been reported that for every drug that comes out of a pipeline, about 10,000 molecules have gone in and got lost somewhere on the way. The average cost of a compound when it pops out of the pipeline is now over $300 million.

The new paradigm is to produce more effective drugs for a wider range of diseases, to make R&D less expensive and to speed up the whole process, and thus benefit from longer patent protection. In order to speed up the process, thanks to technology, companies specialising in individual stages of the R&D process from designing molecular libraries for pipelines to applying for regulatory approval are catalysing unprecedented change. The traditional drug firms are thus able to outsource any part of the R&D process and increasingly do so. Thus are emerging the embryos to help create new ways of doing business in the industry.

The first embryos appeared in the 1980s with the rise of firms such as Amgem, Genentech, Chiron and Genzyme. The success of these companies was based on a technology, then newly developed, called recombinant DNA. Synthesising therapeutic proteins in the *E. coli* bacteria or from the ovaries of Chinese hamsters proved to be hugely successful. This spawned over a thousand pharmaceutical-biotechnology companies all over the world. The main attraction was that these companies became the providers of new molecules to the pharmaceutical companies, molecules made by newer, faster and cheaper molecular biology rather than traditional chemistry. This development spurred the now well-known human genome, government-sponsored project. There also are now a couple of other companies who run their own human genome projects using new techniques to win the race to complete the task at a much faster pace. The sort of information being gathered by these companies is immensely valuable to pharmaceutical companies. Some 20 pharmaceutical companies, including those controlling nine of the world's top ten pharmaceutical-research budgets, have thought it worthwhile to sign up for access to this new information base emerging from the genome project. What all these companies are buying into is a developing model of how human bodies work at the molecular level – indeed an exciting prospect.

There are several such emerging inter-firm formations in the pharmaceutical industry which provide a glimpse into the way that innovations in medicine will evolve. To cite another example is the discovery of the DNA chips, as a diagnostic tool to unravel the relationship between genetics and disease in order to predict who is at risk of what. Screening of new drugs is also now being more and more farmed out to companies like Convance which have developed the new DNA chip technologies driven by software and supercomputers.

The transformation in the pharmaceutical industry, as described in *The Economist* article, is illustrative of what is underway, to a lesser or greater extent, in many other industries. Probably, the IT and pharmaceutical industries are the leaders in creating a new paradigm for business-driven R&D in industry. Two factors, the Human Factor development and Organisational Mindset – will be decisive in distinguishing those companies which will adorn the list of the *Fortune 500* in the next 10–15 years and those which will be left behind as casualties of the 20th century.

Appendix I:
Creating a Project Proposal

Screening of ideas and review of priorities[47]

As has been mentioned, whether in basic science or in technology development or new innovations, the flow of ideas is almost a continuous one. The formal process of capturing and reviewing new ideas flowing via IT networks is undertaken either in a central R&D unit or in an operating company, depending upon classification under science and technology or new innovation. Screening committees recommend those which are of relevance to ongoing programmes and business strategy. In the few instances where ideas may appear to be of a breakthrough class, these are subjected to further in-depth scrutiny and review with businesses, where appropriate.

Project priorities emerge following decisions at annual business-R&D reviews. Priorities of innovation projects are entirely the product of business strategy and plans. The other guiding factors include chances of success compared to commercial value, status of supplying science themes and technology clusters and so on. Project priorities can and do change following scrutiny and feedback by project teams.

Generating a project proposal

Draft project titles or themes emerge as a first step, following the annual round of business-R&D review and decisions thereof. The second step is the assessment of resources for the new project list *vis-à-vis* the status of ongoing projects. Project leaders and project teams are then nominated and assigned to new projects by senior management in R&D and operating companies.

A project leader and the project team members convert a project idea assigned to them into a *draft project proposal*. Such a draft proposal provides the basis for holding a project workshop. In such a workshop, a professional facilitator helps a number of project teams to assess all the sub-elements of their project and to define the eventual outcome. As the final output of such a workshop, a project leader and the team produce a *formal project proposal* together with its costs and eventual reward for submission to the stakeholder or the 'owner' of the project. Following discussions between the stakeholder and the project team, if agreement to proceed is reached, a *project proposal contract* is finalised. Such an approved contract signals the official commencement of work on any project.

Elements of a project proposal

Although the format of a proposal will vary between different firms, within the same firm a common format is considered of great value. What follows is a generic description of various elements which go into developing a project proposal, which may be modified to suit business requirements.

Background

Project title

Project class, for example basic research, technology development or innovation

Fit with business group strategy

Objective of the project

Regulatory or other external issues, if any

Competitive advantage, supported by market data

Current state and future scenario of competitor(s)

Justification

Basic premise of the project

Scientific background and rationale

- Weaknesses in current products/services *vis-à-vis* market opportunity
- Market justification – potential market size
  – possible market penetration
- Nature of project – incremental
  – platform
  – breakthrough
- Patent status

Resource requirement

- Human resources – Training format
  – Expertise profile
  – Manpower
- Technical resources – Scientists
  – Engineers
  – Scientific services
  – External validators
  – Product manager
  – Market research
  – Supply chain and so on
- Physical resources – In R&D laboratory
  – In operating company
  – Outside the company
  – IT network
- Financial resources – Capital investment, if any
  – Revenue expenditure

Time scheduling

- Time plan chart
- Milestones/decision points
- Critical success factors

Evaluation

☐ Risks specific to the project

☐ General risks

☐ Financial analysis – return on investment

☐ Potential to raise market share

☐ Attractiveness of project

☐ Probability of goal realisation

Steps leading to a project contract

Following a two-day project team workshop, a fairly detailed project proposal emerges containing elements described under 'Elements of a project proposal' or some variations of these. To launch a project, the following is undertaken:

Launch

☐ Presentation of project proposal to stakeholder

☐ Modification to proposal following stakeholder's inputs

☐ Stakeholder's approval of project contract

☐ Commence project work

Review of milestones

☐ Competitive status

■ Outlook for next planning period

☐ Marketplace status

☐ Progress of risk management

Project completion and launch

Prelaunch status

Supply-chain issues

Launch MR plan

Ramp up investment and time plan

External validation

Contingency plan, competitive reaction

Main launch timetable

Document total process, including launch and postlaunch performance

Reassign project team members

Project termination

Review failure to meet targets

Likely delay in milestones

Likelihood of failure

■ Assess impact of termination *vis-à-vis* competitors

■ Document total process with detailed account of reasons and cost of termination or delay

Reassign project team members to new projects

Appendix II:
The Business-driven R&D Process

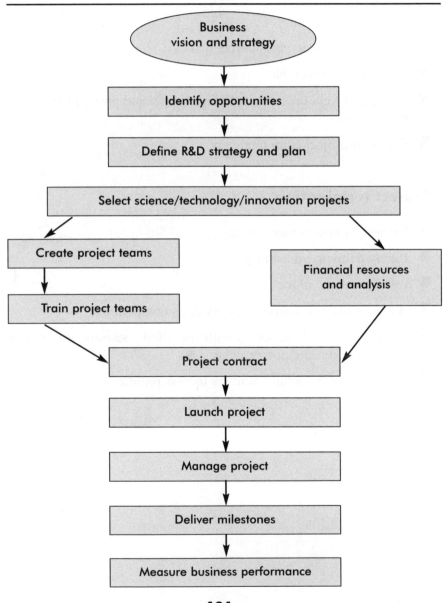

Appendix III: Managing Risk – Targets for Project Teams

Weaving risk into the innovation process

- identifying high-risk projects
- bolstering the quality of gate information
- supporting gatekeepers' structured assessment criteria

Screening and appraisal

- evaluation specification
- product appraisal plan
- appraisal portfolio

Structured risk management

Identify risk ⟶ evaluation assessment

control ⟵ reduction

Tools and techniques

- identification checklists
- risk assessment
- critical evaluation issues system
    - Eindhoven methodology
    - hazard analysis
    - what if analysis
    - decision-tree analysis
- risk education
    - tracking and contingency planning

External contacts and credibility

- external contacts plan
- credibility plan

Fundamentals of project management

Briefing projects Defining team structures Establishing clear leadership

References

1. Grandstand Ove (1994) *Technology Management and Markets*, St Martin's Press, New York.
2. Smith, B L R and Barfield, C E (eds) (1996) *Technology R&D and the Economy*, The Brookings Institution and American Enterprise Institute for Public Policy and Research, Washington DC.
3. Bozeman, B, Crow, M and Link, A (1984) *Strategic Management of Industrial R&D*, D C Health and Company.
4. Cookson, C (1998) 'The R&D Scoreboard', *Financial Times* (Europe), 25 June.
5. Solow, R (1957) Technical Change and the Aggregate Production Function', *Review of Economics and Statistics*, **39**: 312–20.
6. Denison, E (1985) *Trends in American Economic Growth,* Brookings, Washington DC.
7. Mansfield, E (1991) *Science and Technology Yearbook,* American Association for the Advancement of Science.
8. Brooks, H (1994) 'The Evolution of US Science Policy' in Smith, B L R and Barfield, C E (eds) *Technology R&D and the Economy,* The Brookings Institution and American Enterprise Institute, Washington DC, p. 15.
9. Nelson, R R and Romer, P M 'Science, Economic Growth and Public Policy', ibid.
10. Boskin, M J and Lau, L J – 'Contribution of R&D to Economic Growth', ibid.
11. Hall, B H 'The Private and Social Returns to R&D', ibid.
12. Cozens, S E 'Quality of Life Returns to R&D', ibid.
13. Mansfield, E 'Contributions of New Technology to the Economy', ibid.
14. Roussel, P A, Saad, K N and Erickson, T J (1991) *Third Generation R&D*, Harvard Business School Press, Boston, MA.
15. Buckley, J V (1998) *Going for Growth*, McGraw-Hill, New York.
16. Steele, L W (1988) 'Selecting R&D Programmes and Objectives', *Research and Technology Management,* **31**(2).
17. Ibid. (1989) 'Managing Technology', McGraw-Hill, New York.
18. Drucker, P (1988) 'Management and the World's Work', *Harvard Business Review,* Sept–Oct, p. 65.
19. Morita, A (1987) 'Technology Management will be the Key to Success', *Research and Technology*, **30**(2): 12.
20. Hamel, G and Prahalad, C K (1989) 'Strategy and Intent', *Harvard Business Review,* May–June, p. 63.
21. Wiesner, J B (1988) 'More R&D in the Right Places', *The MIT Report,* April, p. 3.
22. *The Economist* (1998) 'The Rebirth of IBM', 6 June, 97–100.
23. Downes, L and Mui, C (in press) *Unleashing the Killer App,* Harvard Business School Press, Boston, MA.
24. Nonaka, I and Takeuchi, H (1995) *The Knowledge Creating Company,* Oxford University Press, Oxford.

25. Gibbons, M, Limoges, C, Nowotny, H, Schwartzman, S, Scott, P and Trow, M (1994) *The New Production of Knowledge,* Sage, London.

26. Smith, B L R and Barfield, C E (eds) (1996) *Technology R&D and the Economy,* The Brookings Institution and American Enterprise Institute for Public Policy and Research, Washington, DC.

27. LINK and Foresight Programmes (1997) LINK Directorate, Department of Trade and Industry, London.

28. Von Hippel, E (1976) *Research Policy*, **5**(3): 212–39.

29. Ibid. (1988) in 'The Sources of Innovation', Oxford University Press, Oxford.

30. Weinberg, S (1993) *Dream of a Final Theory*, Hutchinson, London.

31. Drucker, P F (1993) *Post Capitalist Society*, Butterworth Heinemann, Oxford.

32. Toffler, A (1990) *Powershift: Knowledge, Wealth and Violence at the Edge of the 21st Century*, Bantam Books, New York.

33. Quinn, J B (1992) *Intelligent Enterprise: A Knowledge and Service Paradigm for Industry*, Free Press, New York.

34. Reich, R B (1991) *The Work of Nations,* Alfred A Knopf, New York.

35. Drucker, P F (1998) 'Knowledge and Learning' reproduced in *The Economic Times*, 6 June, Mumbai, India.

36. Levitt, T (1991) *Marketing Imagination*, Free Press, New York.

37. Thurrow, L (1992) *Head to Head*, William Morrow, New York.

38. Hamel, G and Prahalad, C K (1994) *Competing for the Future*, Harvard Business School Press, Boston, MA.

39. Taylor, P (1998) 'For Leading IT Companies, it is Research or Die' in *Financial Times*, 2 September, p. 1.

40. Wheelright, C S and Clark, K B (1992) *Revolutionising Product Development*, Free Press, New York.

41. Wheelright, C S and Clark, K B (1995) *Leading Product Development*, Free Press, New York.

42. Andreeva, N (1998) 'Do the Math – it is a small world', *Business Week*, 17 August, p. 77.

43. Halman, J I M and Keizer, J A (1994) 'Diagnosing Risks in Product-innovation Projects' in *International Journal of Project Management* **12**(2): 75–80.

44. Vergano, D (1998) 'Buy, buy, buy – top companies get rich out of basic sciences', *New Scientist* **159**(2148).

45. Mandel, M J, Foust, D, Farrell, C *et al.* (1998) 'The 21st Century Economy', *Business Week*, 31 August.

46. *The Economist*, 21 February 1998.

47. Turner, J R (1993) *The Handbook of Project Based Management*, McGraw-Hill, Maidenhead.

Index